34/24

GLORIOUS DISARRAY

Glorious Disarray

THE CREATION OF A GARDEN

Joyce Robinson

Illustrated by Ann Swarbrick

Introduction by John Brookes

MICHAEL JOSEPH
London

MICHAEL JOSEPH LTD
Published by the Penguin Group
27 Wrights Lane, London W8 5TZ, England
Viking Penguin Inc., 40 West 23rd Street, New York, New York 10010, USA
Penguin Books Australia Ltd, Ringwood, Victoria, Australia
Penguin Books Canada Ltd, 2801 John Street, Markham, Ontario, Canada L3R 1B4
Penguin Books (NZ) Ltd, 182–190 Wairau Road, Auckland 10, New Zealand

Penguin Books Ltd, Registered Offices: Harmondsworth, Middlesex, England

First published 1990

Filmset in 12 on 13 pt Lasercomp Garamond
Printed and bound in Great Britain by
Richard Clay Ltd, Bungay, Suffolk

A CIP catalogue record for this book is available from the British Library

ISBN 0 7181 3320 X

Contents

Contents

Colour Illustrations

Acknowledgements

First and foremost, my thanks and appreciation to Alan and Sarah Wilson who gave me the inspiration and thereafter edited and presented *Glorious Disarray* to the publishers. I am greatly indebted to Alan who has so generously given his time and expert knowledge. I thank all my family for their forbearance and encouragement, especially Margaret Ann for her patience and hard work in unscrambling and preparing the script from my tapes, and for her delightful sketches which add so much to my book and give me great pleasure. My thanks also to Nada Jennet who gave me confidence to make a start, to the Editor of the *West Sussex Gazette* in which many of my articles recently appeared, and to John Brookes for the Introduction.

Introduction

BRITISH HORTICULTURE is unique in having a long tradition of extremely well-informed practical woman gardeners. I say 'woman' as opposed to 'lady' gardeners purposely, since there was, and still is, a main stream beneath that of the landed gardener. 'Yeowomen gardeners' could they be called? For it is they who have had their own feet very firmly on their ground, and their own hands in it. Margery Fish was in this tradition, Beth Chatto most certainly is there, and so too, I believe, is Joyce Robinson.

Much of the experience of these women has been collated over most of their lives, since gardening is an obsession for them. Their travel is to other people's gardens, their luggage is for plants, their reading is of catalogues and gardening books and ultimately their writings are often in the form of notes or jottings on their observations, winter and summer, wet or dry, wherever they went.

But their real passion, of course, is for their own garden, to which they bring the sum total of that experience and in which they experiment and explore with combinations of plants in the settings which their sites provide; though these are far from sacrosanct and they too receive the improver's hand.

Joyce Robinson has been working on Denmans for forty years, and although incapacitated latterly in its practical running, has by no means given up on its future, and in this I believe that she is unique, for although I have been involved with the garden for ten years now, and inevitably making alterations, she has remained constantly enthusiastic about them. Nature gave the garden an enormous shove in the storm of October 1987, for by losing so many of the trees which Joyce had planted, the garden was opened up to all sorts of on-going possibilities.

One of these, I think, is a far wider concern for the look of plants throughout the year. It is very noticeable in the shots in *The Englishwoman's Garden* by Alvilde Lees-Milne and Rosemary Verey, in which Denmans was included, that few locations were shown without the tumbly summer appeal of the cottage garden. Denmans, however, has a winter beauty as well, which is far more vigorous than a garden of only roses and perennials. For it has bones, and a structure of evergreens and winter colour that make it beautiful at all times of the year. This sort of planting needs foresight.

The use, too, of gravel as a ground medium makes Denmans an interesting all-round garden, for it was planned with a continuity of growing surprises, which poke their unexpected way through its surface, and in which they ultimately seed and propagate to create at all times a jungled profusion of texture and form as well as colour.

This spontaneous plant combination includes grasses and herbs as well as shrubs and perennials growing in this manner, and I believe points a finger at the way of future gardening. For our increasing concern and interest in the environment, its flora and fauna must also be echoed in the inevitable, smaller garden. Yew hedges and formal borders, which are our current concern, divide the garden from their environment and create an alien world and enclosure from it. Can we afford this introspection?

The new garden look can, of course, still create its own idealised natural world, but need it be such a formalised and disciplined way? Joyce Robinson has contributed enormously by loosening up this Edwardian ideal in her garden at Denmans, allowing the public to see its ordered confusion, with which they seem to empathise; for the combination of gravel with random planting has the added practical appeal of lower maintenance too. 'Though it should be informed,' I can hear Joyce admonish. It is that information which Joyce Robinson seeks to impart in this book to a new generation of gardeners, ensuring a continuity of thought through personal expression which, when combined with practicality, keeps the craft of the English garden so alive.

John Brookes
Clock House
Denmans
West Sussex

PART ONE

CREATING DENMANS

Beginnings

THINKING OF THE GARDENS I have made and of the trials and joys through those years of apprenticeship, I find it is the happy things that I remember most, not the hard work and the disappointments. My first garden was at Eastergate Manor in Sussex, where I went to live on my marriage in 1925. It was a farmhouse one, well sheltered with lovely old walls, mature yew trees and a kitchen garden. It stood in a quiet farmyard setting with the parish church and an ancient granary on staddles – and I took it all for granted, for I was

7

just twenty-one. We were farming and I soon found all the outhouses filled with mushrooms and the kitchen garden with choice bulbs and plants being grown commercially. I was given lovely plants but had not the slightest idea what they were or their needs, so I planted roses of many different habits and colours, which grew into an unmanageable mass; I made a so-called rockery with unsuitable stone on ground that I had not cleared of perennial weeds . . . But, nevertheless, I made a garden, despite being very busy helping to run the farms and our nursery business, and having four daughters, the last of whom was born in 1932. By the time the first bombs of the Second World War were dropping we had moved to a smaller farmhouse, where I made a wartime garden of vegetables and fruit with poultry for eggs and meat. During the hot summer of 1941 I grew nearly four tons of outdoor tomatoes. Being on the coast meant there were a lot of other things to do: guarding the beaches at night with only a reduced wartime farm staff and trying to grow two blades of grass where one grew before. I only had a little flower garden there but lovely old apple trees with mistletoe, and somehow the war years passed and it seems impossible now to think we had a box of Molotov cocktails by the back door. How glad we were that we did not have to use them!

By 1945 we had decided we wanted to move to a cottage, but one not too far from our market gardening business's glasshouses. Just nearby was Westergate House, with its cottages, stables, and farm buildings six miles east of Chichester, which had been left uninhabited before the war and then commandeered by the WRAF (the girls in the control room at Tangmere). The farm and the garden had been neither cropped nor fed and everything was very dilapidated. It was just what we were looking for. We acquired the estate and moved into a gardener's cottage.

Those post-war years were busy ones with rationing of all kinds of course, and the scarcity of building materials hit us particularly badly: we waited months for roofing materials (not to mention fertilizers and seeds) and three years for the flooring for our new room. We had to use Sussex flint from my sister's house, which had been bombed in 1942, to build the one room for which we could get a permit.

In those far-off days the cottage was as important to me as the garden is today, for it was from there that everything started. Originally it had been a bothy and then the head gardener's dwelling. It stood in an old apple orchard, surrounded by a walled garden complete with a Victorian conservatory. The whole garden sloped gently south on a free-draining, slightly alkaline soil. What more could one want? Here then was my canvas – although I did not realize its potential at that time, nor what we should be able to do with it. We sold Westergate House and called the rest Denmans, and here I made my third and last garden.

The battle was on, a battle for survival which, if it had not been for my husband, would have been lost. Without his great vision and tremendous encouragement to all the family and to his employees Denmans would not have happened. An indomitable optimist, I think he looked on the reclaiming of the land and garden at Denmans (three and a half years of weeds and wartime neglect) as a project for the family to tackle together. And as well as the land, getting normal life going again after the upheaval of the war years meant a great deal to him.

So there we were in this unexpected place, with its atmosphere of an earlier age, its stables with a clock, a coach house, a lime walk in the park and a cedar of Lebanon planted about 1800; a cricket pitch for the staff with a pavilion and a donkey-pulled roller to go with it. It was so different and so empty and run down our difficulty was to know where to begin. We were anxious not to spoil its simplicity so we left the head gardener's room, the potting sheds and shabby glasshouses with their broken brick floors just as they were, and we covered the walls with peaches and Victoria plums which did very well. There were a few old pear trees near the cottage – I remember how the blossom cheered us after that long winter of 1947.

In 1946 Bertie Reed, who had worked for us at the
Eastergate nurseries since he left school, as had his father
and brothers, was demobbed and started working at Denmans – and he is still with us. With his wife he made his
home in North Cottage on the farm and his first job was
to clear up: what bonfires we had, for Denmans was then
a wilderness of waist-high weeds ... At first he helped
with the stock, the farm hedges and the weeds; then, as
he gradually reclaimed the garden, he started growing
strawberries – literally tons of them! In 1948 we put up a
Dutch light structure and in it Bertie grew salad crops, and
in the walled garden early strawberries, which we marketed

with our other produce. We fed lavishly with cow manure, mulching in the autumn and letting the worms do the work. For the London market we grew paeonies, *Lilium regale*, Dutch iris, scabious and pyrethrum. The battle was won, with a great deal of hard work but a lot of fun too.

In 1950 I realized I had to do something more about the garden, and I began to plant among the strawberries and flowers that we were growing to sell, and thus over the years I gradually laid the foundations of the garden that you can visit today. The different elements of the garden are described more fully in the following chapters.

The Gravel Garden

IN 1969 I WENT TO GREECE and the Greek Islands
and there I found my pattern and my inspiration for part of
the garden I was to make. I had been looking for some time
for another texture, another medium other than grass and
paving and on Delos I found it.

Delos is an island of delight: warm air, blue sky and a
gentle breeze. When we sailed away I was the last person up
the gangway, I was so reluctant to leave. The whole island
was just covered with flowers. All the plants and climbers
one knows so well growing in the land to which they
belong, cascading over and through ancient urns and pillars,
down deep wells and water holes, covering steps and the
stairs to homes long forgotten. Seedtime and harvest *meant*
something here. Everything grew in hot dry gravelly soil –
and in many places just in stones. That gave me the ideas I
needed.

It was a long time before I found the gravel that I
thought right for my garden. If possible you should use
gravel that blends with the walls and the stonework of your
house, water worn and well coloured and not from an
inland pit that has been graded and cut by machine. I was to
find a gravel garden very accommodating and labour saving
(see *Gravel Gardening*, page 46). Of course weeds will grow
but the annuals are easy to pull out and one would not start
a gravel area if infested with perennial weeds. I have no
straight edges to my plantings so I can vary the shapes and

groups of colour and the pattern of the flowers or leaves by running the gravel into the plants or popping a few further out into the gravel. Quite large areas of gravel sparsely planted with a background of small trees with interesting bark can make a quiet place to put a seat. *Acer palmatum* 'Senkaki' has bright pink stems all the winter and the leaves colour well; *Euonymus planipes* and *E. alatus* would make a satisfying October picture. Be careful not to clutter such a space, a few plants chosen to give interest around the year are sufficient.

Have bulbs for all seasons, of course, starting with snow-drops and crocus, then cyclamen and *Chionodoxa luciliae* which seed everywhere without fail, daffodils and tulips of all descriptions, both early and late, in large clumps of one colour to fit in with your evergreen design. *Gladiolus byzantinus*, alliums, *Amaryllis belladonna*, *Galtonia candicans* and the Kaffir lily *Schizostylis coccinea*, sternbergias, fritillaries and many more. Small blue hyacinths under trees make a good picture. I plant tall growing bulbs such as *Crinum* × *powellii*, preferably the white one, lilies, some alliums, and wild gladioli which seed everywhere and can be a nuisance among shrubs or under a wall.

Taking out unwanted wood and deadheading is continuous but with care a lot of flower heads and coloured stems give a later show to the garden. We seldom stake anything: my aim is always to plant so closely next to other plants that they will give support as well as complement each other in colour and form. My garden is supposed to depict glorious disarray. I sometimes wonder if glorious is the right word . . .

The Walled Garden

THE WALLED GARDEN was originally the soft fruit
garden of the old estate. The walls built of flint and brick
are about eight feet high, mostly topped with a damp course
and finished with a slate and brick coping. They stand the
weather well. In 1946 the garden was a tangle of broken
fruit cages and the walls were covered with old trained fruit
trees: pears, peaches and apricots, which meant yet more
clearing up for Bertie. Having cleared the walls we squeezed
in the David Brown tractor and ploughed the whole garden,
paths and all, full of that first fine careless rapture that you
experience when planning or planting a new site but that
you can never quite recapture. For the next year or perhaps
two, while thinking what we would do with it, we grew
anything that would sell – self-blanching celery, Dutch
irises, early strawberries – and continued with market-
garden crops until 1970 when I decided such hard work was
getting too much for us, so we gave them up altogether and
Bertie turned to vegetables. He laid out a conventional
vegetable garden – peas and beans properly staked, parsley
and herb edges, the lot, much more than we could eat and
not enough to market! Herbs seemed to be the answer to
make less work so, in about a third of the garden, I planted
both culinary and medicinal herbs together with many herb-
like plants to give height and substance. These I planted in
the well-prepared soil and covered the whole lot with
water-worn gravel. I did not have the time to look after a

traditionally planted herb garden so everything that I thought would go with herbs was given a place in the walled garden and encouraged to seed thus: by pulling out the unwanted plants, be they weed or herb. A picture was built up that gave a long flowering season and all the herbs that were needed in the kitchen.

However, I still had the greater part of this walled garden and the walls to plant: another adventure, and this time into a whole world of plants, different plants, unusual plants, plants for all aspects and of many textures and habits. First I considered making a garden with raised beds and perhaps some sculpture, then I thought of water and reflections of fish and dragonflies . . . but in the end I decided plants were my love, not masonry. It was not to be a collection of herbaceous plants in borders or island beds; I was thinking of a profusion of growing beauty. Beauty of shape and winter colour, the walls festooned with roses and clematis in irregular groups of colour, beset with winding paths and a few small trees to provide some shade. For trees I chose a free-standing apricot for its shape and beauty of spring foliage, a strawberry tree for its pink trunk and interesting flowers and fruit that are produced together in the autumn, a very small-leaved eucalyptus and a *Robinia pseudoacacia*

'Frisia' planted so closely that they grow through each other. This walled garden faces nearly due south and has openings on the north, south and west sides. In warm weather it gets very dry and strong winds tend to flow around the walls and damage the climbers; but mostly it is a joy, very quiet and still with a remote enclosed feeling, and as it is closely planted and overflowing seems bigger than it actually is. In high summer it is transformed into the enchanted garden of one's childhood. And the walls: they are planted and inter-planted with so many delightful things on both sides that added colour and interest can be found by just peeping over! Wisteria touches the ground on both sides and *Clematis orientalis* grows up, over and into everything. *Magnolia grandiflora* untrained makes a good patch of dark evergreen well above the top of the wall and is host to *Campsis* × *tagliabuana* 'Madame Galen' on one side and *Vitis coignetiae* on the other. Given careful cut back to keep the shape in the autumn and a top dressing of cow manure at least every three years they will grow on in good health for ever. I use no artificial manures, even for the roses.

The 'Stream'

HAVING GIVEN UP all market crops and slipped into just gardening, in 1977 I sold our herd, which meant that Bertie was now full time in the garden. It also meant that a small calf paddock within the walled area was now unused. Here was another challenge, another canvas: I thought of nothing else for weeks. I walked it by day and by night and planned so many different gardens, so many different enchantments for that piece of ground. The perfect idea came quite suddenly and out of the blue. Why not a dry gravel stream bed? I wanted water in the garden but water gardens of any size need a lot of attention and I had firmly kept that idea as only a dream. Why not give the impression of a stream without the water itself? I decided there were to be two dry streams and a water hole – no water at all. Bertie and I marked out with the tractor the design in the grass. The stream is about six feet wide and only a few inches deep, wandering down a shallow slope for a hundred yards or so. On the highest parts I put large pieces of sandstone and ironstone from the Rother valley and boulders of sandstone in the stream itself. Then I covered the whole area with water-worn gravel from the sea bed, which I got from the dredgers in Littlehampton. In one place I put a large flat water-worn stone across the stream as a stepping stone to reinforce the illusion and remind myself and others that it was supposed to be a stream.

The water hole through which the stream flows is about

thirty feet wide and circular. Around the perimeter we threw up a low bank of soil to form a channel which was left unplanted to emphasise the flow of water. Larger rounded sea-bed stones were thrown up unevenly against the plants and the bank and we planted only things that might be found growing in a dry stream bed: grasses, iris, thistles, mint, willow and elder. Under the banks and in the gravel everywhere I planted violets, water forget-me-nots, musk and lamiums. It was all very exciting.

The Conservatory

WE HAVE MANAGED to keep the old conservatory in fair condition although it is nearly 100 years old. It is twenty feet by sixteen, paved and gravelled, with an eight-foot bench for pot plants and two smaller benches. In high summer it is overflowing with things one just cannot do without. On urns or on pedestals are geraniums, begonias, fuchsias, the everlasting *Helichrysum petiolatum* 'Aureum', lobelia, *Thunbergia alata* (the black-eyed Susan), and small clambering climbers such as morning glory and maurandias; in the winter, bowls of hyacinths and other small bulbs. Lilies, eucomis and yellow and white marguerites stand in pots so that they can be conveniently moved about to complete a picture. There is not nearly enough room on the walls and roof wires for all the things I would like to grow. We fill it up completely. *Cassia corymbosa* covers a large area and must be cut hard back every autumn. *Rosa banksiae* and *Lippia citriodora* will both grow outside but give of their best and early in a little heat. The small strawberry guava is good throughout the year; it is evergreen with small bright silvery leaves and clusters of cream flowers that set small round black fruit which ripen well and are delicious to eat. Through it grows a lovely white single *Clematis* 'Comtesse de Bouchaud', a variegated fatshedera and an evergreen wall plant, hibbertia. On the end wall a pinky-purply passion flower grows up and over it all to the roof wires.

The big cold house beyond the walled garden in which

we used to grow early strawberries is a Dutch light structure. New Zealand and other plants that need no heat but shelter from winds and late frosts do extremely well. About 1970 I covered the stanchions and the roof wires with many beautiful plants as well as the ground. We also hold plants in pots to go out later. A lovely place in which to work in March and April, it became an absorbing interest and gives ideal growing conditions for young plants and seedlings. I will discuss its use in more detail in the section about *The Cold House* (page 54).

The Future

IF YOU ARE BUILDING a home with gardens – be they kitchen, flower, herb, water or rose garden, large or small – then you must continually look forward to the time when you have to pass it on. What to do with it? This plot of yours must be cared for by somebody else, but by whom and when? It is a difficult decision. Do you let the weeds grow around you or do you boldly put yourself in a flat and try and forget it? At Denmans the solution has been most successful. In 1980 John Brookes, garden designer and architect, converted the stable block into his home and called it Clock House, from where he runs his practice and design courses. When Bertie and I retired in January 1985 John took over the garden and has built up a well-stocked plant centre. He has also converted the milking parlour and loose boxes into a country shop and tearoom. Denmans is essentially a private garden but it is open from March to October and we have many garden visitors.

I am continually being asked how I started my garden and people question me about my first planning and planting and wonder whether it is as I meant it to be. My answer to the last question is yes, although of course the garden is always changing and maturing. It has taken forty years so far and is going strong! As I get older and slower I am grateful for the trees we planted when we were younger, not really expecting to see them in their beauty. I believe that whatever happens one must look back with joy: the

PLAN OF THE GARDEN TODAY

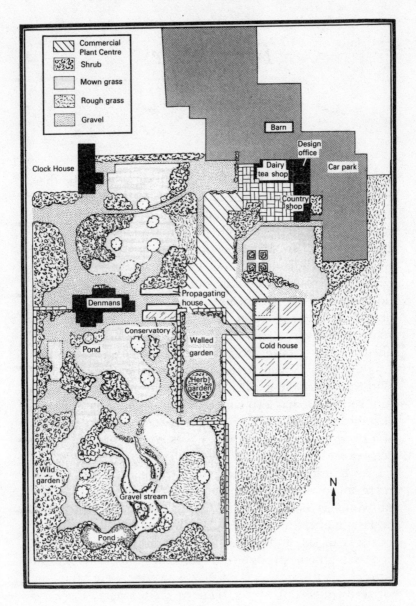

great thing is to be glad not only to have had the chance to use one's creative gifts – be they ever so faint – but also for the help and encouragement one received along the way. Gardeners are a friendly lot. I have been lucky in my plot and my fellow travellers and, after all, one cannot have two forenoons in one day.

PART TWO

BASICS

The Garden as a Canvas

SEPTEMBER IS THE MONTH of butterflies on Michaelmas daisies and buddleias, of lovely still windless days and blackberries on the hedges. In the garden, it should be a time for satisfaction, but it is also a time to think of new ideas and better plantings. It's the time when you need to take stock: one of the gardener's basic skills is the ability to think in terms of the overall canvas. To be able to see ahead in your mind's eye is a real gift of artistry and not something that can be easily acquired. Happily, many people are endowed with this gift!

To some people, a garden is just a collection of growing things around the house which must be kept tidy; to others, it is a joy, their very own interpretation of shape and a leafy fragrance they would like to be able to paint. Perhaps the gardener is more fortunate than the painter or sculptor because his mistakes quickly grow out and are soon forgotten. It is, of course, the plants which make the picture but the would-be artist, the gardener, with his chosen materials, must first prepare the canvas: unless the plants he has chosen like his soil and conditions, nothing can make that careless mixture of colours and textures he ultimately needs.

It takes a lifetime to learn to place and grow your garden plants and trees both for today's enjoyment and for their full potential beauty twenty years on. Surfaces are as important to the gardener as they are to the artist, those on which you walk or those on which your plants grow. They give a distinction to the whole, for different surfaces need plants of different growth and habit. Herbaceous and shrub borders should, I think, be closely planted: by August, with no earth showing at all, the whole is a flowing surface of colour. The plants that are flowering in late summer are of generous proportions, overflowing and all growing together – for the days are getting shorter and the borders are nearly over.

Steps and walls are surfaces that just ask to be planted and suggest the design and shape of the whole garden. Matt surfaces of cement and man-made aggregates do not catch the light and shade in the same way as natural materials, but a garden of gravel is interesting in sunshine or rain, reflecting movement and shadows as sunshine does on a water garden, and in wet weather the stones are a warm brown. A lawn is a surface needing care and attention but, if well-kept, can be so good that it is often admired as much as the flowers and makes a wonderful setting for borders and trees. Long grass with wild flowers and honey bees, or a water garden with lilies and pebbles, needs only a gentle breeze to set the whole surface rippling. So from the entrance gates, the drive or pathway or steps, the house and garden walls, the whole surface of lawns and beds, can all be of growing beauty in some form. The garden is ready for the artist's picture.

To Plant Well is to Design Well

THERE IS A LOT OF INTEREST in design and in the differing use of plant materials in gardens today. To achieve a good design, and therefore a pleasing pattern of growing things, a gardener should try to understand the basics of the artistry with which he is working. The shape and texture of your plantings are the very foundation of good garden design. People tend to forget just how good a really well-planted colourful border can be; random rows and a hotchpotch of plants and shrubs do not make a garden that gives year-round satisfaction. Even with the 'wild-wood' type of garden which has become very popular, the gardener must remember that in trying to copy the beauty of a natural hedgerow or meadow, only those plants which like the particular soil pH and other garden conditions should be chosen.

In the garden proper, design is all important. The size and shape of your borders will be governed by the paths you make and where they lead to; but even more by the plants you grow. The windbreak and the outbuildings, the potting shed and the childrens' sandpit should all be considered within the ambit of planning and planting. It is only by observing the growth and habits of the plants you would like to grow – often by your own and other gardeners' mistakes – that you learn to place plants correctly (but remember the country of origin of an untried plant will give clues to its needs).

The brighter colours of autumn flowers, such as dahlias, need to be placed in front of or near to something that has strong depth of colour to show it to advantage; but the pale shades of midsummer need quiet tones of leaf and foliage: astrantia and penstemons, lilies and roses, all the soft grey Mediterranean plants such as ballota or ozothamnus, look well with creamy feathery things and light soft greens. These can be of choisya and finely-cut foliage of some roses and eucalyptuses, and the purple rhus or *Sedum maximum* 'Atropurpureum'. Bold foliage plants in your borders will provide definite 'full stops' between different colours and planting patterns. Acanthus is good for this. *Phormium tenax* in August, with its flower spikes seven feet high or more, planted with giant thistles and *Verbascum broussa*, provides a marvellous architectural element. A balance must be found between a solid background of larger shrubs and trees (which give shelter and help to form a microclimate) and the light beauty of paler flowers and foliage. It is your choice of suitable plants in relation to each other and to the stronger lines of house, steps and pathways which together make up the whole design.

So far, so good! But I seem to have taken it for granted that the site has good soil and is level. What, I wonder, would I have done with deep clay or a high water table or forty-seven inches of rain a year? Now, with experience behind me, I would enjoy grappling with the problems of a sheer rock face or a rushing stream – even a disused gravel or chalk pit! As the children say, it's easy when you know how. However daunting the prospect, the thing to re-member is that your garden would then need to be planted in sympathy with the whole natural scene. I stayed once with friends near Loch Damh in the Glenshieldaig Forest on the west coast of Scotland. They had been there for many years so the garden had grown into the highland background and really become part of it. There must have been many hazards and difficulties during the winter, but we were there in early September and there were roses

everywhere. Their house was far enough away from the loch to have good soil, but there was also a peaty bog garden down near the boat house. My friends had patiently solved the problem of harmonising their garden with nature, and the result was heaven indeed!

In a different environment, I have seen slabs of slate being cut in a quarry in Wales with groups of pink thrift growing in the cracks up the mountainside and they formed a perfect little garden. I have often thought that large black slabs of slate at the bottom of a stream (always of running water or it would lose its blackness) with pale shades of pink, blue and purple flowers at the water's edge – *Dierama pulcherrimum*, the angels' pink fishing rod, lady's mantle and grasses – would be delightful.

But back to earth! Many of yesterday's tools and sheds which are no longer used can be included in your design just by thoughtful planting. Stone buildings, an interesting roof or a potting shed are wonderful places for climbers. I have an old round grinding stone on a dilapidated wooden frame: with a *Fatsia japonica* beside it, and standing in bluebells and daffodils, it makes a perfect spring picture, but also looks right all year round. Some years ago we took down a lean-to glasshouse and capped the walls with stone. After laying a herringbone brick floor, it made a home for some of the more tender plants. The golden hop is a good climber which covers many yards of roof during the summer and it only needs cutting to the ground in the autumn. *Clematis tangutica* and *C. orientalis* need the same treatment and ivies, if controlled, are perfect for introducing a subtle gleam of silver or gold up an old conifer. Linking together any buildings or garden walls into an harmonious whole with your home, by careful planning and planting beautiful growing things: that is the intangible thing we call design.

Know Your Soil

PEOPLE OFTEN TELL ME that they have impossible soil. They have sand, clay, stones and everything, it seems, except what they want and I suspect most of them just put up with it. But there is no such thing as impossible soil. It is what you make it. If the balance has been upset in any way – by the builders perhaps, or rotavating in very wet weather, or the drainage impaired by panning – it is difficult to get it right again. Often it must be left fallow for at least a year to allow nature to right herself. But if your soil has been badly treated and you do not know how to deal with it then seek good advice. It may not be nearly as bad as it looks. As a gardener, I think that the site and the soil is of the utmost importance. It is possible to change your rooms and fittings and even roofs and entrances but your environment and its soil will always be with you.

You can of course change the soil – it is very time-consuming and will need constant attention to give satisfaction, but it is possible and many people do it. We have a wonderful example at Highdown near Worthing in Sussex where the late Sir Frederick Stern made his garden in a disused chalk pit. When I was about sixteen I remember lying on the top of the old pit on Highdown and looking down into it and seeing the holes ten feet or more deep. They were filled with compost and refuse, and topped up with good soil. His first plantings were silver birches and sorbus which, being successful, he followed with magnolias and many other beautiful trees. Miss Gertrude Jekyll, in her book *Wood and Garden*, tells how she removed donkey-cart loads of soil and refilled with garden refuse and leaves before planting *Lilium giganteum* bulbs in two feet of enriched leaf mould.

Of course, it is in theory possible for ordinary mortals to do what Sir Frederick and Miss Jekyll did, but that was early in this century and things are very different now. However, there are many ways of growing the plants you wish to have, so do not be dismayed if you find your soil difficult to manage. I knew a gardener so keen that she learned how to make compost correctly before she planned her new garden, which was of deep clay; she used a lot of shredded newspaper and vacuum-cleaner dust added to the organic materials she collected. If you can get it, there is nothing like farmyard manure; hop, mushroom and even wood shavings all make good compost – but it must be well made.

Particular environments can of course be created. Two-foot high parallel walls of peat blocks eighteen inches apart and infilled with an acid soil mixture is an ideal place to grow the lovely things, such as rhododendrons and azaleas, that must have these conditions. Wide, shallow steps made of bricks or wood laid in a sandy limestone mixture or a rubble base makes a wonderful home for lime-lovers. The relationship between soil pH and plant growth is extremely complex, but the choice of worthwhile things to grow is so vast that there is not much point in struggling to grow subjects unsuitable for your chosen patch. If you are prepared, however, to put a lot of thought and careful work in the preparation and planning for any rather special-choice things, it becomes an on-going joy – for there is so much to learn. So, consider your soil and its needs, for of all things with which the gardener has to contend, it is paramount.

Paths

PATHS SHOULD ALWAYS LEAD directly to anything
of special interest in the garden, or people will take short cuts
across your beds! In large gardens, really wide grass paths
through plantations, or between herbaceous borders, are
gracious and make a lovely setting for tall border plants.
Mown rides circling through areas of longer grass give an
illusion of space, and can lead on to wild gardens or farmland.

However small a garden, the paths should take you on a
voyage of discovery, preferably going through, or by, your
different special plantings. Make your path of gravel or
stone if they are to stand up to hard wear; grass soon looks
patchy if much used, and a dry path is especially appreciated
if wide enough to walk and talk with a friend.

In really small gardens, the path leading to the bonfire
and rubbish heap or to the garden shed must be wide
enough to take a wheelbarrow, and the garden shed itself
can be covered with honeysuckle, clematis or roses. There is
no need to make your paths of expensive hardcore, unless
you are on very soft ground or the water table is high. Level
and roll it well, making it a little higher than the beds to
allow for drainage, then cover with fine gravel – preferably
water worn.

Brick paths, either plain or patterned, laid in sand only (no
cement), always look right and are a joy to make. Flagstones
and old bricks – if you can get them – or modern paving

stones and cobbles from the beach, or even ashes, edged with blue flowers of course, all blend quickly into the garden scene. A well-made dry path is good in all seasons – and gives much satisfaction to the maker. Curve all your paths and lawns so that your eye leads on to something else, just around the corner.

In a large garden, steps of stone or brick, really broad and shallow, make a grand entrance to a rose garden or down to a lake or an orchard. So, if your garden is on a slope or you have problems of different levels – steps are the answer. To look right, they must be constructed with care, and any stone used should match your house colour. Steps can be quite inexpensive to make on any slope, however steep, but care must be taken to use suitable and good materials. On a slight slope, the steps should be very wide and very shallow, with railway sleepers or split pine logs for the 'risers' and between them use gravel, which is readily available, for small alpines and tiny shrublets.

Walls

THE WALLS AT DENMANS are one of our chief assets. The walled garden was built about 1820, the same time as the house. The other walls are not so old and are of London brick instead of flint, and they are not wearing so well. I have learned to make deep plantings in front of the walls and to cover them with an abundance of climbers and good wall plants to form a continuous flowering, from the gravel at one's feet to the top of the wall. In such a place width of bed is more important than length: fifteen feet is a manageable width.

Anyone can buy plants, but it is positioning them happily together, mixing their colours and shape of leaf and texture, that makes a satisfying planting. One such planting at Denmans, in front of a wall facing west, is made up of quite solid things. Over them grow light, airy climbers, giving a touch of 'icing on the cake' and making it a complete garden in itself, well furnished and smelling sweetly. The bed is about fifteen feet deep and thirty-two feet long, with a stone seat against the wall, and at one end an arch opening into the walled garden. The bones of this planting are an *Osmanthus delavayi*, an elegant small-leaved evergreen very sweetly scented; three *Rosa rugosa* – 'Scabrosa', chosen for its magnificent hips as large as tomatoes; then 'Roseraie de l'Hay', a lovely deep purple with good hips; and 'Frau Dagmar Hartopp', pale pink and large hips. Next is a *Fatsia japonica* with ivy-like leaves all year and in October erect cream

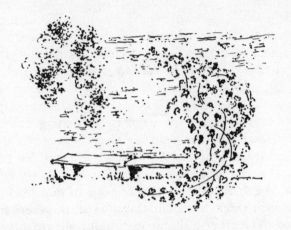

flower heads; an *Osmanthus* × *burkwoodii*, a sturdy and strongly scented evergreen shrub for the end of the border; then an evergreen *Hebe* 'Henri Defoss', a deep violet blue. Together they make a good robust planting – strong enough to carry the climbers.

On the wall itself are two climbing roses – R. 'Caroline Testout' and the old-fashioned R. 'Ophelia'. For a backcloth to all and sundry I use *Vitis henryana*, a small-leaved creeping vine that clings to the wall and colours well in the autumn, and is easily controlled by pulling away any that is not wanted. A *Clematis montana* 'Elizabeth' planted the other side of the wall hangs down and over the roses, and the rampant growing *Vitis heterophylla* is covered in the late autumn with aquamarine-blue, grape-like fruits in clusters, quite beautiful. In the gravel at the base are *Hosta sieboldii* and *H. decorata marginata*, *Euonymus radicans* 'Emerald 'n' Gold' and *Verbascum broussa* which forms silver rosettes on the ground all the winter, and five feet stems of silver grey all the summer. I call them my men from outer space.

In the angle of other walls facing south and west, I have made a home for some smaller things: *Omphalodes verna*, *Lithospermum diffusum* 'Heavenly Blue', lewisia and androsace. Having no rockery to hold them, I find they get lost in a mixed border. So, instead, starting right in the corner, you could make a brick floor in just sand, no cement, from wall to wall as deep as you wish. It is interesting and simple to form a pattern, herringbone perhaps. Next place a railway sleeper, or two if necessary, then flagstones or gravel, then another sleeper, thus forming an acceptable area for planting in between the flagstones, and down over the sleepers. Mine is on a gentle slope, so the sleepers form steps ending in grass, but your plan can suit any shape you wish. If it is larger, then leave more space between the 'risers' for gravel. Among your plants leave a definite pathway to the seat in the sun in the corner.

The wall behind this seat will be an ideal spot for wall plants and climbers that like to be hot and dry. For autumn colours and larger leaves, plant an ornamental vine, *Vitis coignetiae*. You can also rely on many of the clematis, fremontodendron, or a good ceanothus and through them all a white *Solanum jasminoides* 'Album', a semi-evergreen which flowers for months. An evergreen or two at the base of the wall gives shape and background to your small plants on the pavement. *Choisya ternata*, *Pittosporum tobira*, an osmanthus or a daphne would be suitable. When making your choice for the pavement area mix evergreen and deciduous plants with careful thought for their winter appearance. For height and colour above the walls, planted whichever side of the wall is convenient, I have various eucalyptuses that I cut back yearly to keep them only a few feet above the wall. Over and through one climbs the final touch, a lovely *Rosa banksiae lutea* which has clusters of double yellow flowers and likes its feet in the cool on the north side and its head in the sun.

A happy knack with doors and doorways, entrances and vistas are all important. Grand entrances through iron gates to stately homes and castles are often magnificent, but everyone's house and garden, however small, can have a gracious and welcoming entrance. A curved drive or path to the front door is pleasing. An arched doorway into the garden is inviting, and, if occasionally left open to show a colourful vista, gives joy to friends and passers-by. If one is lucky enough to have walls, then openings through them can be of interesting shapes and sizes. A complete circle of iron, like a cartwheel, creates a lovely peephole into a walled garden. Iron gates or strong wooden doors within an arch enhance any garden wall, whatever its surface, and even quite low walls and fences can be made beautiful by thoughtful planting. To have a view of hills or mountains, to a lake or over farmland, is the prayer of every garden maker, but a vista can often be contrived by the intelligent placing of shrubs and small trees.

To Mow or Not to Mow

A Flowering Meadow?

FOR MANY YEARS it has been important to most people that their lawns should be mown at least once a week and preferably at weekends. Now the fashion is for longer grass, and even longer with wild flowers growing in it. The result can be very beautiful but I have certain reservations and do not recommend it to everyone: so much depends on the setting of your lawn and garden. However, in a carefully planned garden it is possible to have both long and short grass, giving yourself less mowing and the opportunity to create another growing picture with a completely different range of plants, adding interest and variety to your gardening chores. Lawns around the house, and your main paths leading from it, should I think be mown. They make a good setting for the house and provide space to walk and talk with friends. To get the best of both worlds I suggest that your main mown path leading down the garden should be as wide as possible and curved. This shows off your planting to perfection – but remember it should always lead to something interesting.

If you are making a new garden or starting a new area of longer grass from scratch there are many good mixtures of grass and flower seeds available from reputable merchants to suit your particular soil; or if you have some rough grass that you mow only once or twice a year that would be very suitable for your new little flowering meadow. You need do little to the rough grass but cut it and introduce suitable new grasses and wild white clover. If there are perennial weeds such as large tufts of docks or nettles these can be killed with a spot or a well-controlled sprayer. Having cut the grass, leaving it about eight inches high, and having killed unwanted clumps of perennial weeds, it is a good idea then to give it a dose of organic fertilizer and wait for rain. Having achieved a healthy crop of grass, the next summer or early autumn is a good time to sow perennial flower and grass seeds and follow in March with some annuals. Be sure you know the soil pH to enable you to order the correct seeds for the soil.

All that is fairly easy; it is the mowing at the correct times that is the difficult operation, as all haymaking needs sunshine or at least fine weather. The first crop of grass should not be cut until the seeds of the early flowering plants (such as your buttercups, moon daisies and white clover) have dropped and then all grass must be removed. I say 'crop' as it can be used either for fodder for a pony or goat or as compost, but in either case it should be dry before it is picked up. This is always a gamble: if the hay is to be used as fodder it must be covered when dry and tied down as the Scottish crofters do; but preferably it should be put in an airy shed or barn. If it is to be composted, dryness is not essential but makes it much easier to handle.

So, during the first year just cut and fertilize and cut again if necessary, but leave the grass not more than five to eight inches high. In the second year, you will enjoy the flowers in the meadow and you should cut and remove all the grass when the seeds have dropped. Cut again in early autumn after the grass seed has dropped. The important thing is not to let it get too long and out of hand, but not to cut all the heads off before they have dropped seed for next year.

If this little meadow can be situated at the far end of the

garden, it could end with a border of ornamental grasses six feet high or more which can be cut right down in the spring or winter. The whole would look well if fenced and could have a small gate opening on to the mown grass path back to the house and garden.

There are many ways one could lend interest to such a meadow. Three silver birches in the corner or a few crab apples – *Malus* 'Golden Hornet' and *M.* × *robusta* fruit every year with good leaf colour late. Remember also that this little meadow need not necessarily be in the country – it could be in the heart of a busy little town.

Water Gardens

AWATER GARDEN is a very personal expression of
artistry and can be the crowning glory of a well-kept and
well-stocked garden. It is often made not just for the actual
water effects – although they can be beautiful – but as a
home for plants that need such conditions. 'Damp but not
wet' calls for clever planning. It is easy to pop in water lilies
and such, that do not mind being totally immersed, but it is
much more difficult to get summer colour and good brown
winter stems growing naturally near the water's edge, without looking overplanted.

If your water garden is to be man-made rather than
based on a natural lake or stream, then your design must be
well chosen. Do not lose sight of your first inspiration, and
be careful to use only materials that complement your house
and surroundings. There are two basic themes: a pool or
canal made of brick and perhaps some stones; or a curved
and rounded natural area of water in grass and or gravel.

There is much to be thought of and carefully planned before one starts. Unless well understood, the actual digging
and shaping of your design, and the sealing of the bottom
and sides in the material of your choice, are better left to
specialists. One always thinks a stream that does not dry out
completely in the summer to be ideal, and they can be lovely,
especially in the spring. But everything grows *so* fast that in
such conditions weeds are difficult to control. One small piece
of running grass or water buttercup can cover your plants
in a week.

One can cross a lawn or cut grass to reach the informal water garden, but the brick-made pool or canal may be reached by gravel and brick paths. Here, containers and jars can hold agapanthus or lilies, and be gay with flowers most of the year. In many ways the formal pool is easier to maintain. It needs only pockets of different sizes to be left in the brickwork and filled with soil for your planting. Around this formal pool could be a brick patio and beds of roses would not be out of place – it may well be the centre of your outdoor activities, for sunbathing, a barbecue, a place to sit with your friends.

The site for either is most important. It should not be so near deciduous trees and shrubs that their falling leaves are a nuisance. In size it should be comparable with the shape and size of the whole garden, and look as if it had been there for ever. It should have fish, dragonflies, water lilies and of course a seat.

Essentially your informal garden of water is planned for quietness and peaceful contemplation and should be away from chatter and business. It can be a place of real beauty and contentment.

Gravel Gardening

I HAVE RECENTLY HEARD from gardening friends in Pennsylvania who are making a gravel garden. They saw mine a number of years ago, when it was first at its best and their letter reminded me of those exciting days when I discovered gardening on gravel.

One reads of Victorian, French and Italian gardens, knot, herb, wall and paved gardens, woodland and rose gardens ... but gardens are whatever and wherever one makes them. Flint walls wired and planted but not so completely covered that one cannot see their beauty are gardens in themselves. A patch of celandines and aconites in the middle of a wild paeony that I collected in Portugal gives me a wonderful spring picture; I can control only the celandines – I dare not disturb the paeony. If allowed to seed within an allotted space, many combinations of plants make complete little gardens of their own. The marble leaves of *Arum pictum* with the evergreen Gladwin iris make an attractive pair, as do hardy cyclamen under a tree in the orchard. Hebridean crofters' gardens may be only a few carefully tended herbs barely a foot from their doors, but are gardens nonetheless. Bulbs also can be used in this way: aconites, scillas, bluebells and daffodils; later in the year alliums, galtonias, *Gladiolus byzantinus* and in the autumn nerines, Kaffir lilies and colchicums. These self-sown patches of beauty that occur every year first gave me the idea of a

garden in which I could walk dry-shod among my plants.
That was in 1969 and in April that year I found my
inspiration on Delos where flowers grow profusely between rocks and ancient walls and steps, and all in gravel
and stones.

So I made a gravel garden using water-worn gravel from
the sea bed. We are on well-drained soil, my plot was
well manured and workable so it only needed to be levelled
and rolled. I used a strong rake and a small garden roller
in good weather conditions and walked on it well. Gravel
gives another texture and finish in place of the usual paving
and grass, and planting can be done before or after gravell-
ing as the plants become available. A good site is among
small trees and shrubs; it gives shelter and character to
groups flowering at different times. I was lucky to have
enough space and that feeling of stability necessary for the
planting I made among full-grown ornamental cherries,
silver birches, large *Viburnum plicatum* 'Mariesii' and *Hydrangea aspera* and *H. villosa*. Under a mature Young's weeping birch and a snakebark maple are some daphnes and
many variegated and other shrublets.

Twenty years later we have removed a dead *Arbutus unedo*
'Rubra' and many overgrown shrubs which were obscuring
the view down to the fields and after rolling and regravelling
all is now prepared and we are back to the original design
and ready to plant again. Having learnt over the years about
many new plants – some that are not too hardy – that we
now hope we can grow in the gravel, having established a
suitable microclimate, the possibilities for a colourful design
and display are endless: old-fashioned double primroses,
masses of hellebores, *Chionodoxa luciliae* and, of course,
forget-me-nots and violets everywhere. Epimediums, euphorbias, clumps of erythronium, *Omphalodes verna*, *Salvia
argentea* and a lot of grey and purple. In the shade I would
like *Kirengeshoma palmata*, *Liriope muscari*, *Veratrum nigrum*
and small ferns. It will take some years to come again to
perfection but the basis is there.

A Labour-saving Garden

CAN YOU SPARE three or perhaps four hours a week to tend your garden? Would you like it always to look well cared for and full of colour? All this is possible – provided it is a well-designed small garden and that you work to a plan. Briefly, this plan should be no digging, no containers or pots, and to grow masses of biennials and self-seeding plants.

The unjust steward complained that he could not dig and to beg he was ashamed. But today, he would be told he need not beg if he could not dig: he could grow all his flowers and most of his vegetables without that effort – the organic way. Most people firmly maintain that they must dig their gardens and, if growing a rotation of vegetables, there must of course be a reasonable depth of workable soil to enable the developing roots to carry the food to the plant. But it is a fallacy to think that digging is essential to good husbandry. Certainly the soil must be kept open and friable, but this can be done by mulching heavily in the autumn and allowing the worms to do the work.

My first choice of a good mulch would be rotted cow manure or well-composted garden refuse. Either of these mix easily with other natural matter such as lime, soot, wood ash, dried blood, fine brick chippings or sandy grit. It is not likely that pig or poultry droppings will be readily available, but stable sweepings, although somewhat bulky to use, are suitable – especially if left for a year to rot and then mixed with garden compost or peat.

An ideal labour-saving garden is so closely planted that there is no room to dig. In the autumn, it can then be completely covered between the plants with an animal or garden compost. My own garden has been built up on cow manure; we had the cows and so for forty years we have used little or nothing out of a bag.

Having decided to allow yourself time to sit and enjoy your garden, the design must give you as much satisfaction and beauty as the flowers – so it should be very simple and easy to work. How is all this to be done? The final choice of design must be yours, of course, but I suggest that, to keep the work down, there should be no grass. Instead, for walking with friends or as a patio, use small water-worn gravel. A few flagstones or old bricks set in the gravel show off your flowers well and can be used in many ways. Think of a wide curved path of gravel through two deep borders of shrubs and plants; or a half moon or complete circle from your house and patio – surrounded by deep continuous plantings in which you can grow just as much as you can manage, and so that it all looks right from any angle. As your garden is based on compost, you will need a gravelled area of about twenty feet square for a tool shed, a wire cage for making the compost, and space to burn whatever refuse is unsuitable for composting. To be

accessible, this area could be behind or close to the garage and screened by evergreens.

I am still thinking of a small garden, so the borders will completely fill it: a few small trees at the back to give height and shelter, then flowering shrubs, some evergreen, and through them all, masses of perennials and biennials. So there will be no bedding plants and, of course, no mowing; no edges to cut and no machines to keep in order!

Since my own garden was designed to depict glorious disarray I grow many varied self-seeding plants. This does not mean that it is an untidy garden – although sometimes I think that 'disarray' overtakes the 'glorious'! – but one that is so well stocked with perennial plants and shrubs that the whole growth is controlled by elimination rather than planting. There are many good things that seed themselves with abandon – so go carefully with the hoe: it is difficult to see what you have destroyed before it is too late! Hand weeding on gravel after rain is easy work and you can leave drifts and colonies of small plants to bloom in the following year. We all know how forget-me-nots and poppies will take over your garden, so get some unusual seedlings going as well – and not only summer ones. In January and February the green hellebore (*Helleborus foetidus*) will be showing bloom, and in March and April there will be pink, white and blue violets among the early primroses with heartsease, forget-me-nots and sweet rocket. Soon – everywhere and all at once – the gravel will be covered. It is the larger summer biennials that give you the colour and height, in the border and along its gravel edge. The taller ones extend your flowering season so there is always something about to burst into flower.

After a year or two, the foxgloves will be marvellous. Two good ones are the strawberry-pink *Digitalis* × *mertonensis* and *D. ambigua*, which is shorter and yellow. The campanulas are prolific – *C. persicifolia* and *C. latifolia* are quite different in character in blue and white. *Verbascum broussa*, with its tall spikes of soft yellow, has woolly grey leaves that lie on the gravel all winter and make a delightful picture – but look out for the slugs! Tall herbs look wonderful in the summer border: the fennels and angelica, *Salvia sclarea turkestanica*, astrantia and lady's mantle, and Miss Willmott's ghost, *Eryngium giganteum* and poppies, poppies everywhere. The small yellow Welsh poppy starts in April and will be with you most of the year. Next come the musks, dead nettles, and cheiranthus, the small perennial wallflower; later, the Kaffir lily, *Schizostylis coccinea*, and *Dierama pulcherrimum*, the angels' fishing rod. At the back of the borders, for height, you can use the Scottish heraldic thistle *Onopordum acanthium*, a giant but very picturesque. Just let everything grow together. You may think it will make more work, but, after all, you have had no planting, no pricking out of plants: everything has just arrived, and when they have dropped a little seed for you for next year's disarray, just pull them out and put them on the compost heap to make the mulch to feed the worms to enrich the soil to grow the plants that make your beautiful garden!

Small Greenhouses

A SMALL GREENHOUSE is very much more difficult to manage than a large one and calls for constant care and ingenuity if it is to be successful. If the house is not over-filled, and one is not too ambitious, it is possible to create beauty and have a lot of fun. A greenhouse – perhaps twelve by six feet? – in which you grow tomatoes and a few cucumbers, and can raise some bedding plants if you like, can be attractive as well as functional and useful.

Three well-grown tomato plants, planted in March, will give you the early fruit. Then follow with an outdoor crop – if you need them – on a south wall in growbags, which, if covered with peat and stones, will look part of the garden. Cucumbers can be grown just as well in a frame or even on the compost heap! A good one is 'Femina' which gives you no male flowers. I would suggest no specific bedding plants, but why not sow annuals in late April *in situ* in all the odd spots outside instead? And then, if you have any bare soil left by the end of May which you must cover, buy a few good plants for immediate colour.

You now have a house in which to have fun, with a work bench four feet by ten inches or less – on one side only, with a small propagating box leaving room for pots of cuttings and growing-on space. A narrow shelf nailed on to the back of the bench is useful and keeps the soil and pots from falling off. Put a few paving stones in front of the bench on which to stand; then cover the rest of the floor with gravel, and you will have one side of the house as a gravel and paved area in which to plant your beauty.

Gather a large pot for geraniums, two hanging baskets and a slender climber or two: morning glory, *Clematis macropetala*, an abutilon or the black-eyed Susan would be suitable for such a greenhouse and can be controlled. A roof climber, tied to the wires, would give shade in hot weather – preferably one you can cut right down in winter – but not plumbago, *Jasminum polyanthum*, a vine or a peach, for all of these would soon run out of control.

In the gravel floor, you can plant an agapanthus, an arum lily, ferns and very small ground-cover plants, such as a small-leaved ivy or *Ficus radicans*, things that will not grow too big. Under the bench, you could have more ferns and so on – but always leaving space to hold things that are over; or you could have boxes of early mint and parsley.

Between the tomato plants, until they cover the ground, you could start small boxes of lettuce, courgettes and runner beans to put out at the end of May.

To make a complete unit, a grass-fronted 'lean-to' shed with a bench under the window, facing south, is a joy for starting your potatoes or dahlias; and it is somewhere to hang the onions and shallots or to grow on your potted cuttings. In fact, your 'cubby hole' ensures that the greenhouse need not be cluttered, so leaving room to sit sometimes and do nothing! If you then made up a good deep frame of Dutch lights – preferably near the greenhouse – and had a stand pipe and hose long enough to reach your frame, what more could you want?

It sounds simple doesn't it? And it is. But be careful not just to buy everything you think might do, or feel you must keep your friends' cast-offs, or you will soon have your greenhouse overrun with things you do not want.

The Cold House

A Garden of Tender Plants

IN VERY COLD WEATHER, it is the freezing wind that causes most damage to half-hardy shrubs and plants. Those from California and New Zealand especially like just a little shelter to do really well. Even if correctly secured, so they do not rock, the young branches and leaves of ceanothus, myrtle, eucalyptus, pittosporum and even rosemary and lavender get very bruised in our south-westerly gales. The shelter of a wall, or even better a thick evergreen hedge, helps; but it is worthwhile to encircle or partially protect them with well-staked and secured canvas. A deep well-fitting covered frame will hold many of our precious things like double primroses, choice auriculas and penstemons through the winter. However, a large cold house makes the growing of tender plants possible and it can be very useful as well as decorative.

We have such a house at Denmans, the Dutch light structure we erected in 1948. For forty years it has given many happy hours to many people. It is always a pleasure to work in, particularly in February and March when one is able to do necessary jobs in comfort out of the wind. It is a second-hand cold-frame house made by Frampton Ferguson in about 1930, with a lightly constructed frame of aluminium on a concrete and brick base. The roof and walls are of standard-size Dutch lights slotted into the frame and it is ventilated by hand-controlled roof lights and the removal of frames from the side of the house. There are six bays of ten feet by one hundred feet, with double doors at each end – so that it can be difficult to ventilate in strong winds. In very hard weather, the ground inside freezes, but not deeply.

Having at first grown tomatoes and, later, early strawberries in it the ground was in good heart when, to make less work, I thought of using it as a home for some of my more tender treasures. I allowed myself two-thirds of the house in which to make this garden and, having decided where the paths should be, we rolled and gravelled them. It looked very bare and forbidding and I wondered if I would ever make it look like a garden. I had been given some New Zealand plants, some phormiums and pittosporums, *P. tobira* for one, which is a delightful beautifully scented shrub with yellow flowers and soft rhododendron-like leaves; also the Australian climber sollya and the fragrant Tasmanian jasmine periploca, both of which will reach the roof wires. Soon, however, I was visiting nurseries that grew such plants and found exciting shrubs and climbers to add to the house, all of which were fresh to me – many I had only read about.

I brought in from the garden the evergreen climbers trachelospermum, *Drimys winteri*, *Daphne odora*, and some ceanothus. Up the stanchions, I put the more tender honeysuckles, the yellow *Lonicera* × *tellmanniana* and *L.* × *heckrottii* 'Goldflame', and two double clematis – the mauve *C.* 'Vyvyan Pennell' and the large white *C.* 'Marie Boisselot'. It still looked very bare, but I was soon to discover how quickly everything grew in such a warm, airy and sheltered environment. It needed a lot of water. Passion flowers, morning glory, abutilons and the Banksian roses grew apace. Between the shrubs and climbers, I filled in with Mediterranean and other grey-leaved shrublets. To give some substance, I planted germanders, ballota, the myrtle *Luma apiculata*, which has creamy white flowers, very sweetly scented, and the main stems are a soft pink like the arbutus. I brought in some shrubs and tender salvias and, of course, flowering tobacco (nicotiana), stocks, lavender and poppies. Agapanthus, clivias and other lilies, especially *Lilium regale*, do very well and extend the flowering season, for they bloom a little earlier than those in the garden. For strong leaf shape and background, I planted *Fatsia japonica* and the loquat *Eriobotrya japonica,* and *Lagerstroemia indica*, which in India is a tree, but with us, makes a large bush covered with pinky-mauve chestnut-like flowers every year. It is lovely and was given to me as a seedling by a friend. We also had fuchsias and geraniums in pots and urns as well as hanging basket arrangements. Finding plants for the house is a great adventure into a world of quite different growing things, which I always enjoy.

Meanwhile, in another part of the cold house, Bertie grew some splendid vegetables. A centre path and a bench on one side of the house, with lashings of cow manure on the other, enabled him to grow early and late young vegetables of all sorts: carrots, many varieties of onions, new potatoes and a succession of salad crops. These included tomatoes and cucumbers, and peppers on the east wall. Melons grew on the bench in the hottest corner (and looked delicious, hanging over the edge of the bench). He continued to grow all the brassicas, runner beans and root crops outside in the kitchen garden. There was always enough of everything for everybody and herbs as well – including, of course, parsley and mint. We now miss it all very much: one cannot compare bought vegetables with those freshly gathered from one's own garden.

At a later stage, I started propagating plants and shrubs from the garden to sell to garden visitors. The house was, and still is, an excellent place to pot and hold container-grown plants. I am always encouraging my friends to put up such a structure, not so large maybe, but instead of the conventional small greenhouse which is so often used only in the summer months – and then not to capacity. An unheated house, facing south and against a wall, is, in my opinion, the best house to have. In it one can grow anything: decorative plants and climbers, early bulbs and ferns, with a bench for potting, and room to grow a few bedding and container plants to put out in May.

Wildlife

❦

Of Birds and Trees, Mice and Slugs, Cabbages and Kings

'WILDLIFE' IS AN IMPORTANT SUBJECT for the gardener and our attention has been re-drawn to it very forcibly following the gales of October 1987, since when many of our garden birds and small animals had to change their territories and nesting places. In our case, life at Denmans was further complicated by the experience of the A27 being converted into a dual carriageway at around the same time as the gale. We expected some confusion when the contractors started, for it meant the removal of not only the perimeter hedge and iron railings, but also some mature beech trees and standings of holly twenty feet high. Immediately we had more small birds than before, though, having good garden cover, we always have finches and buntings, robins, grey and pied wagtails and all the tits, including the long-tailed one. A few migrant warblers on their way inland rest in a *Magnolia stellata* year after year; and three times we have had wrens roosting in a huddle in an old coat hanging in the woodshed. Wagtails will congregate in this way in winter – we had a dozen or two one year that sheltered in the cold frame house throughout a snowy period. Siskins and linnets are always with us, and goldfinches – but only when the grass seed is ripe.

I find the bullfinches and the haw and the greenfinches beautiful but very destructive. I would not want to be without the thrushes, both missel and song, or the black-birds, as there is nothing quite like the song of two thrushes calling to each other across the garden. As well as the green woodpecker, we have the greater and lesser spotted ones and the tree creepers. I can only remember seeing the hoopoe once. The cuckoo likes us for our hedges and small trees and in early April I open the door of the toolshed a few inches ready for the first swallow.

So you can imagine that we were rather overcrowded when the trees were cut and the birds changed their habitat. They did not move far, but stayed on the farm and the nearby orchards until moving on in the spring. A bedraggled stray cat arrived and had her kindle of kittens under a shed, which was a nuisance because we could not get at them to feed them and they all became wild – and, of course, took the young birds. There were clouds of wood pigeons on the young crops which we could have done without and we did not notice that the deer and the foxes had moved in until a vixen had her cubs on the nearby Fontwell racecourse. Bert, who takes a great interest in birds, put out some food for the woodpeckers on tins; and night after night, it was taken – tins and all – by the vixen for her cubs. The tins were found on the racecourse. Collared doves and green woodpeckers strolled on the lawn; magpies and jays knew no fear; and there was much fighting for territory.

The October gale came after a busy overcrowded summer. We lost large chestnuts, limes and beeches together with much hedgerow cover and old macrocarpa and conifers in which the birds had roosted. The worst havoc was in the Rewell and Slindon woods which meant, for us, a further influx of homeless birds. The rooks have been looking for their usual trees which are not there, but they have made do with others. There are more jays and magpies than ever before and a sparrow hawk; and, although we have always had rabbits and moles which we could more or less control, and grey squirrels which we could not, this year they are secure in the roots of fallen trees and just sit up and watch us!

It was such a mild winter that year that mice prospered and increased; seventy-one were caught in the toolshed during two weeks. Mice can be a real menace to a gardener and cause havoc among seed trays and dahlia tubers if not controlled. They like to make their nests in the warm soil under the vines in the conservatory. Woodlice and earwigs, which seem comparatively harmless until they get under hard-wood cuttings on the propagating bench, ants and slugs, red spider and aphids: no wonder a gardener needs to watch his plants and seedlings carefully. I wish I could attract

more ladybirds to keep down the greenfly; and other acceptable bugs to deal with all the other baddies – though I
always have doubts whether the right one will win. Anyway,
if you do remove a slug from a lettuce bed, it will go
straight for the freshly pricked-out cabbage seedlings – but
there are always hedgehogs to help. Don't despair. Kipling
said that an English garden could not be made by saying
'"Oh, how beautiful!" and sitting in the shade', and a
garden is not only slugs and weeding, it is beauty, colour
and shape and the joy of putting it all together to make your
own patch. It is also about sharing, for a garden is never
finished – it is just beginning for those who follow.

To Stand and Stare

❧

Developing New Skills

ON A MIDSUMMER DAY, with plants and trees at their best, I have sometimes found that I am not as satisfied with my garden as I should be. What has happened to the good resolutions I made in January? That simple statement of W. H. Davies comes into mind: 'What is this life if, full of care, We have no time to stand and stare?' I know at once that I must do something different and interesting, as well as my garden, for a while.

Although there is much one can do, it is difficult to decide just what it shall be and, being such a personal choice, I hesitate to offer suggestions. As a countrywoman, my own choice would be to learn a country craft. I have always wanted to be able to build a stone wall and to make a garden gate or even a summer house. Well-made brick paths or stone steps are a joy to construct and it would be grand to do it with others and in the proper manner.

If you cannot take time to do such a course, you must find something different to do in your garden. To collect and grow the best of your biennial seed is simple and well worthwhile. Sow them very thinly to save pricking out, in a clean piece of ground. They will make strong plants which can be moved in any open weather until the spring. This plan is especially useful if you have perennial weeds, for it is impossible to clear the ground among growing plants. Your plants will be in great demand at sales and coffee mornings, especially if you have the lovely new foxgloves as offered by Thompson and Morgan! Hellebores are also much appreciated and nearly all grow well from seed – but it is important that your collected seed should not be kept in a bag, but sown as soon as it is gathered. Another task to tackle would be dividing your good perennials and planting them up in rows.

Though I would not wish to do it myself, dried flowers, potpourri, seed heads and lavender bags all make good presents and you have the materials there to use. If you have more fruit and vegetables than you need, then well-made and presented preserves always sell well. Bee-keeping or wine-making are other alternatives – but they can become bigger enterprises than needed or anticipated! They are very hard work and time consuming, but the end product can be very good indeed.

Another garden adventure that could well become a longer-term hobby, and one I have always wanted to do, is to grow young trees. This is only possible, of course, if you have enough, and suitable space. I have often thought of starting such a venture, and native trees would be my choice. You would need to do no digging, so the young trees must be planted sufficiently far apart for the weeds and grass to be mown. Anything and everything may be planted as you collect it and will grow fast if moved with care and kept watered until rooted. Plant them in rows for easier working as you collect them. The ones you would like to see together when fully grown, probably for others to enjoy, should be spaced with careful thought and planted where they are to stay. Gradually, everything that is not needed must be disposed of via gifts, sales, exchange or the bonfire – which will leave room for the chosen ones to grow to maturity.

So 'stand and stare' for a while – it could well be that you will return to your gardening refreshed and looking for fresh fields to conquer.

PART THREE

PLANTING

Learning about Plants

AS I WRITE about my garden plants, I remember clearly the people who first introduced them to me and told me about their habits: people who must have influenced me as I grew into gardening. A small child's interest in flowers is often limited to the daisy chain, but I remember being allowed to pick a handful of St Brigid anemones while gardening with my mother when I was very small, and another time pulling apart and planting pieces of rooted polyanthus. Was that the moment, I wonder, when I started to grow green fingers? That was over eighty years ago and there is still so much to learn.

The years before school, when a child has time to be alone and do little, are important. I made a garden of ferns and stones at the bottom of a damp ditch and no one could think why my shoes were dirty. Although I helped to grow vegetables at school – for it was 1916 – and spent much time with Harry Pearce, our gardener at home, I did not think seriously about plants and planting until 1927 when I had to deal with an unkempt garden and a young family. There was some *Iris stylosa* under an old wall which surprised me when they flowered, and a few old-fashioned rose bushes. I soon became more and more interested in plants and how to grow them because my husband, being a grower, was marketing flowers throughout the year and my whole life was of farming and growing.

I learned a lot from Dora Boniface who was in charge of

the alpines and perennials in Barnham Nurseries near us in Sussex for many years. Later, during the war years, there was no thought of gardening or garden making, except for growing food, so it was not until 1946–7 that I again started visiting nurseries, botanical gardens, R H S shows at Westminster and reading and learning all I could from growers and nurserymen. Mr Beatty, who was a director at Frank Toynbee's Croftway Nurseries (also at Barnham) at that time, taught me a great deal about shrubs and how to place them and also that, as he would put it, 'a garden should never be cluttered'. He was a wonderful plantsman and had worked with a wide range of them all his life. He was also most encouraging and one day, I remember, he brought his friend Mr Finlay, that great gardener from Edinburgh, to see my finished planting of trees and shrubs here at Denmans.

I had many good gardening friends who were remaking their gardens after years of wartime neglect and together we visited nurseries which specialised in unusual and choice garden plants – I used to spend whole days at Wisley. Unhappily, many of those nurseries have gone, for there was great competition from the garden centres. It was at the time when Ken Aslett, whom I knew when he was at Toynbee's, was rebuilding the rock garden, and what a marvellous job he made of it. There were many happy days spent walking at Hillier's at Winchester by myself, with a notebook and a packed lunch, often until the gates had been locked and the men had gone home. I was given much encouragement by Mr Hillier himself and I walked and walked to learn the names of trees and shrubs. At Bressingham I met the Bloom family and found so much of interest in their then new layout of island beds, and from them I learned of yet more plants of which I had never heard. I also visited Sissinghurst Castle, Great Dixter and Higham – where another gardening friend introduced me to Sir Cedric Morris who showed me his wonderful collection of irises; we exchanged hellebores and other plants for some years afterwards.

Looking back over those thirty years, I realize it was no wonder that this would-be gardener was overawed. Having a walled garden ready to be planned and planted, I was greatly impressed with the walled gardens of Winchester and Salisbury, especially the cathedral closes. They were my first lessons in planting and interplanting wall shrubs. The enclosed and fenced gardens of the New Forest and its brown gravelly streams gave me yet more ideas. There I helped my sister make a fern garden in an open ditch using the brown pebbles from her stream and a raised bed of gentians. Treseders of Truro and the Cornish gardens of Trelissick and Trebah gave me further inspiration on the use of tender plants in the Dutch light structure which we were then converting from market crops. But of all the gardens and shows I visited, I probably learned more at Hillier's Jermyn's nursery and arboretum at Ampfield near Romsey than anywhere else. There, I could identify plants I had seen elsewhere and read about. But my thoughts on shape and texture were crystallised while walking and observing nature's way of using colour and variations of height and distance, as in the Spanish Alps and the Ronda mountains, and among the pale soft colours of the flowers and sky in the Greek islands, and the contrasting grandeur and harshness of the Scottish Highlands . . . even the quiet peace of my own Sussex Downs.

Plant Association

PEOPLE OFTEN ASK ME: 'How did you know those colours would look well together?' or, 'Did you get that planting idea from a book?' The answer is very personal: like your clothes or the arrangement of your sitting room, the choice is yours and, although we learn by trial and error, example is, I think, the most helpful.

For those making their first garden, 'putting plants together' can be very confusing and many people are quite at a loss, they do not know even where to begin. Not being familiar with the names of the plants you would like to buy or grow might put a beginner off gardening altogether – but don't let it! Use the common name if you can. Call a forget-me-not a forget-me-not and not a myosotis. But if you know something of Latin or Greek you will find to your delight where some of the proper names originated, and so deduce something of their needs. The more you learn about plants, the more you want to. I have found Harold G. Hillier's *Colour Dictionary of Trees and Shrubs* (David & Charles, 1981) excellent. It has useful pages on the habits or hardiness of a large collection of good things to grow.

I am assuming that you are not making a garden from scratch or are on a new site, but that you have become interested and would like to give your garden a new look. Although you are longing to get on with your garden-making, do have your soil tested. It is simple but important that you should know your pH before you plant.

I have sometimes suggested that a corner or some other suitable small area should be planned and planted first – just to find your feet as it were. Prepare the small patch by forking it over and removing all trace of perennial weeds and adding whatever it needs for good fertility. Choose plants that like your soil and – especially and only – those that you like, not the ones the garden centre thinks you should have. You could plant this small patch up as a small garden complete in itself. As an amusing exercise, why not put it on graph paper, allowing a foot to a square, and cut it to size and shape. Then mark in your trees, shrubs and perennials, herbs or alpines, filling in the spaces on the paper to the size each will eventually be – give or take a bit of course! And draw a gravel path along the front for small creeping things and alpines to grow in.

Perhaps you have a wall or old apple tree you could use to carry a climbing rose or clematis? Work out what you need to make an all-year-round garden: a half-standard crab apple, three or four shrubs, two evergreens, five clumps of perennials with three of a sort in each clump, two 'bowls' of daffs or tulips (not scattered) – and there you are, you are beginning!

There are many ways of planting, but do let the design be yours. Now, having gained some confidence, take another bite – and a bigger one this time. Should you need shelter from the prevailing wind, let your next adventure be a wedge of small trees: three silver birches (*Betula pendula*), two Portugal laurels (*Prunus lusitanica*), two purple nuts (*Corylus maxima* 'Purpurea') and a half-standard sorbus would do.

There is a lot to consider when working out a new garden scheme, but, as I continually emphasise, it must be your choice of plants. I grow a lot of pale colours and have few or no red flowers; but in a dark corner, with only the morning or the evening sun, dark dahlias or gladioli with light fluffy grasses and a bold golden shrub such as *Sambucus nigra* 'Aurea', behind, make a glorious patch of colour for several weeks.

I always think that lists can be very dull, but I can say that I have grown the following plants together successfully: the purple and gold sages go well with the sedums; the Oriental poppies and *Phlomis italica* with hostas and lady's mantle; astrantia with alliums and euphorbias. For low shrubs, the daphnes are good: *D. odora* 'Aureomarginata', *D. × burkwoodii* 'Somerset' and *D. pontica*. Hydrangea species such as *H. villosa*, *H. sargentiania* or *H. quercifolia* can be grown with or near *Rhus cotinus*, weigela and *Philadelphus coronarius* 'Aureus' – all are good early summer shrubs.

For full stops at the end of the border, acanthus, *Fatsia japonica*, purple berberis or *Osmanthus delavayi*; and roses mix well with the small lilacs *Syringa velutina* and *S. microphylla* 'Superba' – neither exceed five feet and they do not sucker.

All these plants are well-tested, beautiful garden shrubs – but you need not get them all at once! I have been forty years maturing my garden and I am still finding new ways of 'putting plants together'.

Annuals and Container Plants

WHEN MARCH COMES ROUND, it is time to take stock of annuals and container plants. If there has been a bad winter, there may be more spaces to fill than usual and annuals may be just the job. An easy way to grow the annuals is to sow thinly in groups in April in the place where they are to bloom. This saves time in pricking out and caring for tender seedlings; and, grown this way, you usually get good strong plants. When thinning, leave only the best, giving them plenty of room to grow and, later, a sprinkling of compost to help them on their way.

There are also simple but beautiful plants which no garden should be without, for example, forget-me-nots, foxgloves and honesty. After some years they need to be invigorated by the introduction of healthy plants from other sources; otherwise, by continually self-pollinating they tend to revert to their wild state. It is important that any plants of a poor colour or form should be pulled up immediately after flowering and put on the compost heap. By thinning and caring for your seeds, sown in the border where they are to bloom, many new strains can be started and all they need is to be top dressed from time to time with an organic manure. You can have delphiniums; tree lupins; *Lavatera arborea*, the tree mallow; potentillas; oriental poppies; and *Lathyrus latifolius*, the everlasting sweet pea, which, if planted near a tree or large shrub in the border will give height and should be cut down every year in the autumn.

To grow something quite different from usual is always interesting, so why not try colourful fruits of, say, gourds, peppers, and sweetcorn, yellow- and red-flowered runner beans, coloured and variegated cabbage and the true castor oil plant *Ricinus communis* for its fig-like leaves; and, of course, some of the new nasturtiums with mottled leaves and pale flowers. It is always a mistake to put summer plants out too early. They hate cold winds and do just as well planted a little later when the fear of frost is over.

Your containers and terracotta pots, filled with fresh compost, look inviting and this is also the time to decide what your theme is to be. There are so many plants from which to choose that there is no need to have just geraniums or begonias. One of the easiest and cheapest ways to vary their look is to use some of the smaller silver-grey Mediterranean plants: the grey and lime-green trailing helichrysums soften the outline of the pots; and among them you can grow annuals and tender plants from your winter pots. If not allowed to dry out, fed regularly and the annuals replaced when necessary, the containers can be kept colourful and different until the autumn.

Spring Plants

NEAR THE HOUSE, in gravel, I have a varied collection of spring-flowering plants under a parrotia tree. The tree itself is always good to look at, having an open habit with weeping branches that turn up slightly; small red flowers grow on the bare branches in March and April – like an elm – and its leaves are pale green and beechlike. In late summer, they turn a lovely colour, rather as if suddenly splashed by a paintbrush. Beneath there are snowdrops, pale primroses, epimediums, erythroniums, variegated *Arum pictum*, two perennial foxgloves: *Digitalis ambigua* and *D.* × *mertonensis*. The green winter *Helleborus foetidus* and a clump or two of *H. orientalis*, the Lenten ones, are all good value for both flowers and foliage. Campanulas, alyssum, thrift, dianthus and grey- and purple-leaved primulas all leave good leafy plants after flowering; and a flat stone or two makes homes for saxifrages, sedums and the tiny soldanella. Keep the snowdrops and any larger daffodils or tulips away from the front of a border because their leaves can be troublesome when over; but love-in-a-mist, perennial wallflowers, especially *Erysimum* 'Rufus' and *E.* 'Wenlock Beauty', and the columbines you must have. Once established, you will have them always.

To furnish the gravel during the summer, *Omphalodes verna* makes small tufty plants and the cloak-like leaves of lady's mantle are lovely after rain. Some of the early perennials also make acceptable places near which to place small bulbs that are so easily lost.

Though one would not be without them, spring flowers do pose a problem when placing plants that are to flower later. However, enjoy every minute of them, for spring is soon over!

Thinking about Roses

WHAT DOES JUNE MEAN to you? To me, it means long soft evenings and an abundance of growth. Everything grows, including weeds! The trees are fresh, eating chestnuts and limes are in full flower, and the roads here are white with 'Sussex lace' and moon daisies; and hedges have hawthorn blossom and wild roses and the garden is at its best. There is nothing to compare with well-grown summer plants. The spring bulbs are neat, colourful and lovely. The ornamental fruit trees are laden with blossom and bees. The lawns look well, the clematis and other climbers cover the walls, and, best of all, the roses are in bloom. Nothing takes the place of a rose!

It is not easy to express one's thoughts about roses: they are so numerous and different. They have been grown and cared for by peoples all over the world since time immemorial; lost, and found again; named and renamed. It is a commonplace but true statement that they are everyone's flower – for cottage or castle.

Few people with gardens, large or small, would wish to be without them; and now that so many are bred small and fairy-like, they can be grown in window boxes and containers too. I have always thought that weeding keeps one humble, but the beauty of the ancient Chinese or Persian roses does so even more. How many centuries since their forebears were growing in a palace garden in the mountains of Asia or the Himalayas?

Roses have been crossed and recrossed until it is often impossible to trace their ancestry. Their form, colour and scents are so diverse that it can only be a very personal collection one can grow; to name any set as the 'best' would be an unwarranted presumption. My own taste is for species and the 'old-fashioned': grown as shrubs – on their own roots, not grafted – up trees and over buildings and walls.

October is a good time to plant new roses, so they can settle before the winter. The best roses are not cheap, so be sure to buy only good plants with plenty of flower buds. Except when planting climbers, or shrub roses specially placed for colour or to complement other plants, use those of the same named variety together, particularly the rugosa and the old China roses. Many species have wonderful coloured foliage with large translucent red thorns; others have round or urn-shaped fruits.

The long fern-like sprays of *Rosa xanthina* 'Canary Bird' make a misty foil to the pale colours in your garden and last for weeks. There are small-flowered climbers with elegant sprays of tiny pointed buds often used in bridesmaids' bouquets and buttonholes. One, R. 'Cécile Brunner', has long growths like fans of perfectly-shaped shell-pink buds that bloom from May to October. Another, R. 'Alister Stella Gray', is a delightful little buttonhole rose with good clean dark foliage and clusters of small slender rich-yellow flowers, deliciously scented. 'The Garland' rose and the climbing 'Little White Pet' both have small bunches of creamy-white flowers which will cover many yards of fence or tree; they need pruning only to keep them manageable.

Roses differ so much in size, vigour and habit that one could spend a lifetime working with them and still wonder at their beauty. Yet their needs are so few: just to be well fed and kept clean! Little enough to give for the abundance of joy they give us.

Good Border Plants

NOT EVERYONE has the urge to look for new plants and indeed most people do not have the time to do so. The true gardener is not necessarily the one who has taken a gold medal at Chelsea no matter how magnificent his exhibit. What is new today may well have been growing in our grandparents' gardens and probably known by a simple local name. Not all good plants are rare or in short supply, but because some plants are more difficult to grow than others, it is often only those ones which are talked about or discussed. Perhaps we do not make the most of those which give less trouble, perhaps we don't place them well or allow them to grow to full beauty. I am quite sure that a border of colourful plants that you like and know is what really makes for happy gardening.

In a garden that is large enough to warrant a conventional herbaceous border, a mixture of fruit trees, shrubs and flowers gives a feeling of controlled disarray that is very natural and satisfying. When I was asked by an American gardener to explain an English cottage garden, I found it difficult; but it could be a comfortable arrangement of fruit, flowers and vegetables. The true cottager would need to use the greater part of his plot for food, so quite a narrow path of grass or brick between borders of flowers and herbs, backed by trained fruit trees, would be the ideal arrangement. For more on cottage garden flowers, see the chapter *Cottage Garden Plants* (page 96). Copying this pattern of

vegetables grown among flowers has recently become popular again. It shows off the decorative leaves of vegetables, complementing the summer flowers. The architectural red-leaved rhubarb, globe artichokes, and sea kale with carrots and beetroot look well in the flower border with the silver-leafed chard, fennel, angelica and always the purple and gold sages. Tall perennial sunflowers, such as *Helianthus decapetalus* 'London Gold', and white moon daisies at the back are magnificent with the many different mints, anchusa, musk, lady's mantle, Michaelmas daisies, euphorbias and golden rod. It is the autumn mulch that keeps them healthy and full of flowers year after year.

There are many excellent perennials that will grow into large plantings if left undisturbed. Acanthus, Japanese anemones, *Salvia* × *superba*, especially the variety 'Lubeca', black-eyed Susan, *Phygelius capensis*, the red hot poker, oriental poppies, flag irises, lamb's ear, pulmonarias and ajuga can all be left for several years – for they look so much better in large patches. Other things which can be treated in this way include the small hardy violet, creeping thymes, sedums and dianthus. None of the plants I have mentioned need staking or watering; just dead heading and a double handful of compost every autumn. What could be easier?

The Flower Border in August

THE FLOWER BORDER in August can look very lush and healthy and the shrubs and perennials have put on a lot of growth. Of course, if the weather has been wet, then the flowers will not last long and the roses may well have a short season. When the first strong colours of summer are nearly over, the quieter tones and paler shades should form a background for the things which are to come. It is a good time of the year to look critically at the flower borders, perhaps making a little room for something new or different?

Definite splashes of white or very pale lime in a border make an eye-catching pattern when looking from your windows or down the garden path. For this purpose, I use *Lilium regale* and *Romneya coulteri* and *Hydrangea arborescens* 'Annabelle' or the white *Anemone japonica*. For the large blowsy clumps of flowers in August the yarrow, *Achillea clypeolata* 'Moonshine', potentillas and the white phlox are all very good. The thistle-like heads of eryngiums (which are a striking metallic blue), the hardy agapanthus and the strange seed heads of *Phlomis italica* all go well together. Large patches of one variety are best if you have room and, between them, masses of soft leafy plants such as anaphalis, Michaelmas daisies *Aster ericoides* 'Horizontalis', *Hosta sieboldii* and the Gladwin iris for its seed pods, lavender, calamintha, the eau-de-Cologne mint and *Artemisia* 'Powys Castle'. A really outstanding bulb for the first week of

August that's easy to grow is *Galtonia candicans* – with a pointed cluster of white flowers on a two-foot stem. There are many small plants that you can pop in front and let run back into a border: liriope; some of the small-leaved variegated hostas; the foliage of epimediums and euphorbias; and there will still be the foliage of the meadow rue (thalictrum) and *Salvia purpurea*, and for a large interesting plant, in a corner perhaps or at the end of a border, acanthus is wonderful.

So although August has the reputation for being a difficult month for colour, there are plenty of good things from which to choose to keep the border interesting. The late flowering myrtle *Luma apiculata*, *Itea ilicifolia* (with long green catkins and bright shiny leaves), feijoa with silver – not grey – foliage and its strange tufts of mauve flowers growing near to *Berberis thunbergii* 'Rose Glow' are spectacular in a sunny corner – and all flower in August. For shape and soft-coloured foliage, August is a good month because your plants have had time to mature to full height and beauty. The phormiums, especially *P. tenax* 'Purpureum', are very showy in August as are *Sambucus nigra* 'Aurea', *Rosa rubrifolia* and *Catalpa bignonioides* 'Aurea'. The mountain paeonies *P. delavayi* and *P. lutea ludlowii* make groups of finely-cut foliage in late summer; so do *Aralia chinensis*, the angelica tree, and the white-stemmed *Rubus cockburnianus* and R. *ulmifolius* 'Bellidiflorus' (which has huge panicles of deep pink flowers and edible fruits). Two lovely climbers for this time of year are *Campsis* × *tagliabuana* 'Madame Galen', the salmon-pink trumpet vine, and *Clematis* × *jouiniana*, but both cover a lot of wall space.

New Life in Your Borders

IF IN DOUBT about how to bring new life into a would-be summer-flowering border, use grey and pink, or grey and purple, grey and blue, or even grey and gold – but never grey and red. Use at least three of a kind of the grey plants, or five if it is a large bed.

Assuming that this summer border already has some tallish subjects to give stability, then run your grey plants back from the grass or gravel edge, leaving space among them for the coloured plants of your choice. Some good grey plants to use are: *Hebe* 'Pagei', *Artemisia* 'Powys Castle', lavender, rosemary, the curry plant and *Senecio greyi*. Then take your chosen-coloured subjects and plant them among the evergreen shrublets you are using to give some shape to the renewed border. There will not be a lot of room, so use good well-furnished plants but do not overplant.

I suggest the following for extra colour in spring and summer: clumps of penstemon; the Kaffir lily, *Schizostylis coccinea*; *Gladiolus nanus* 'The Bride'; *Dierama pulcherrimum*, the angel's fishing rod; *Omphalodes verna*; and *Liriope muscari* – in a little shade; and if you think you need it, and there is room, a few good annuals in large patches: white or green nicotiana is good. If you want daffodils, use large white ones, 'White Sails' or 'White Nile', planted close together as in a bowl. If you have more room, then *Lilium regale* is easy and will stand a little lime; and some iris of good strong colours to enhance your scheme.

'However small a garden the paths should take you on a voyage of discovery ...' Here a path leads past an *Acer platanoides* 'Crimson King' and *Chamaecyparis lawsoniana* 'Fletcheri' towards Clock House in the distance.

Above The Clock House, home of John Brookes who now runs Denmans garden. *Below* Behind the *Prunus* 'Tai-Haku' and *Betula pendula* is Denmans, the converted cottage that has been Joyce Robinson's home since 1947. In the foreground is an *Ilex* 'Golden King'.

The green and gold of mature trees and shrubs at Denmans. Behind the juniper and fatshedera in the foreground, you can just glimpse the gravel stream that winds through the lawn.

'Definite splashes of white in a border make an eyecatching pattern.' *Left* A magnificent yucca. *Right* Foxgloves and verbascum.

Two of the entrances into the lovely walled garden. *Above* Sage, honeysuckle and roses frame the south wall entrance, and *below Verbascum broussa* and *Osmanthus × burkwoodii* guard the west.

Inside the walled garden, 'a profusion of growing beauty'.

Right Rosa centifolia 'Fantin-Latour', catmint, euphorbia, verbascum and pittosporum line the east-facing wall.

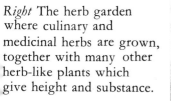

Left A seat in the sun against the south-facing wall, a perfect place to admire a gravel garden.

Right The herb garden where culinary and medicinal herbs are grown, together with many other herb-like plants which give height and substance.

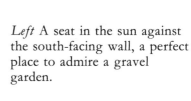

The formal and informal in harmony at Denmans: *above* the ornamental brick fish pond with the conservatory in the background and *below* 'mown rides circling through areas of longer grass give an illusion of space'.

Glorious contrast in colour and form in the flower borders: *above* a silver birch towers over foxgloves and *Berberis thunbergii* 'Atropurpurea' and *below* sage, roses, phormium, loquat and ceanothus against the soft red of an old wall.

Denmans, 'designed to depict glorious disarray', with *Fatsia japonica* and *Euonymus* 'Emerald Gaiety' in the foreground.

Being on gravelly rather alkaline soil, I grow no azaleas or rhododendrons. There is so much that likes our well-drained ground that, if kept top dressed with rotted manure, it will grow anything. Camellias will do well if planted in plenty of peat and sandy grit, and where they get no morning sun.

The hydrangea species, though somewhat naked in winter, are well worth finding. *H. villosa, H. quercifolia* and *H. sargentiana* are quite easy once they get away, and they tolerate quite heavy ground cover. All the hellebores and the perennial foxgloves suit this purpose. We grow early primroses and a clump or two of daffodils under the bare branches, to extend the flowering period.

I find that plants found in the wild mean so much more to me than man-made hybrids which tend to have such top-heavy flowers. I like to know who found them and where: the white hardy cyclamen from Rhodes and the blue poppy from Tibet are good examples – how exciting it must have been! I have two delightful patches of hardy cyclamen under lightly-branched evergreens. They are pretty if grown with small-leaved ivies – *Hedera helix* 'Buttercup' is ideal, or the small silver-edged *H. h.* 'Little White Diamond'.

People are often afraid to overfill their gardens, so they become too careful. If you know your soil, and therefore what it can grow, and know what plants you would like to have, then plant with abandon. There is such a wealth of good things from which to choose, and so many places from which to buy, it is important to buy only good healthy plants. If possible, they should always be on their own roots – not grafted.

If you find you have made a mistake and have upset the balance and design of your established plantings, then do not hesitate to dig experiments up: give them to a friend! Or plant them elsewhere! It is as well to have a nursery plot where you can hold such things until needed; if possible near a water tap to make watering easy.

To get together a collection of good plants, which you hope to live with and enjoy for many years, calls for bold-ness, but the rewards will be enormous.

Late Summer Flowers

IT IS DIFFICULT to keep the borders full of colour after August – though there is still much to come. When the paeonies and delphiniums are over, and the roses; when the herb garden and the lilies begin to look tired, then is the moment when your well-planned late-summer perennials will take pride of place. They look particularly fine when grown with the background of purple or grey recommended previously. The placing of plants to bloom in later summer needs careful thought to ensure good results. The purple *Rhus cotinus* is wonderful by itself in August – but it is even better with species of hydrangea, the foliage and hips of *Rosa moyesii*, a large clump of *Anemone japonica* and something tall, such as *Phormium tenax*.

The blue-green thistle-like heads of *Eryngium giganteum*, known as Miss Willmott's ghost, and *Kniphofia caulescens*, which has large agave-like leaves and peach-coloured pokers, all mix well with *Dierama pulcherrimum* and the white flowers of *Romneya coulteri*. Giants such as *Heracleum mantegazzianum*, the tall cow parsley, *Onopordum acanthium*, the Scottish heraldic thistle, and *Verbascum broussa*, can stand over seven feet high, so self-sown seedlings that are not in the right place must be ruthlessly removed before they get too large.

Dahlias and chrysanths, of course, make a good show, but are more difficult to fit into mixed plantings. Late bulbs give great interest and importance just where you need

them. They can come and go from late July to the end of
September – or even later. *Galtonia candicans*, crinum, amaryllis, sternbergia, autumn crocus – colchicum – and the
hardy cyclamen are all easy and obtainable. For formal beds,
tubs or containers, fuchsias are gay and last for weeks if
kept watered. And so your later summer plants take you
right into the glorious colour of autumn.

Propagating and Caring for
Choice Plants

LATE SUMMER AND AUTUMN is the time to propagate your special plants – those that you would not like to be without. The seed from some salvias, violas and delphiniums, even forget-me-nots and poppies, should be collected as soon as it is ripe if you are to have them where you want them and not just where they drop. Most perennials need only to be divided and offsets replanted, but some may need more care through the winter months to get established. These should be put in pots and held in a frame – or, better still, a cold house – until February or March. I then stand them out under a wall or a hedge for a few weeks before putting them in their place in the border. Some that are better done this way are the border chrysanthemums, the small perennial wallflower cheiranthus, liriope and the hardy agapanthus *Sedum maximum* 'Atropurpureum', asarina (which is a small creeping snapdragon), the herbaceous *Clematis recta*, gentians, francoa – and, of course, there are many more.

A few plants can be really difficult to propagate. Among them is *Romneya coulteri*, the California 'tree' poppy, which will romp away through everything, but when trying to propagate it, I find the only way is by taking root cuttings with two or three good buds and to hold them in pots of open gritty soil until they have filled the pot with roots; and only then to put them out in the border. This may take two years or even more. Another is *Helleborus niger*, the Christmas rose, which needs quite different treatment from the other hellebores. It is better left in a pot for at least a full growing year. I put three small pieces, with roots, together in a pot and let them grow into a good strong plant before putting them out. *Yucca filamentosa* and some of the less rampant grasses grow best from side shoots held in pots as do the small hostas and *Anemone hepatica* and *A. pulsatilla*. Sometimes it is easier to take the seed, but to be sure of getting the true variety, it must be a cutting or a piece of the original plant. Even more difficult, but still worth the extra care is *Cimicifuga racemosa*, which gives a patch of white in the border in September. Others are *Tropaeolum speciosum*, the scarlet climbing nasturtium which likes a damp place and grows profusely in Scotland, the old double primroses, the double mauve meadow rue *Thalictrum dipterocarpum* 'Hewitt's Double' and *Convolvulus cneorum*. Do not be put off by the names: they are all obtainable and well worth growing.

August and September can be busy months for taking cuttings. The soft-leaved Mediterranean plants are best taken at this time for they root quickly and, when potted up, usually safely overwinter in a cold house; the same can be said for ballota, the artemisias, helichrysums, *Salvia* × *superba* and *S. ambigens*, geraniums and rock roses. It is a good time to insure against losing alpines, sedums and other small plants such as gentians by potting up a few. After a hard winter, to find some of your treasures safe and sound is a real bonus. Finally, before tucking up for the winter, make sure there are no woodlice or ants where you are going to store your plants because they can cause real havoc under small pots.

Ground Cover

I AM OFTEN ASKED to recommend suitable plants for ground cover – but a low massed planting just to cover the ground means different things to different people. In many gardens, there are places which are difficult to include in the overall garden design. An exposed position may well be covered with wind-resistant shrublets or prostrate evergreens to protect something else that is growing on. There are many possible situations and solutions. A glimpse (but not an entrance) through a tall evergreen hedge or a shrub border, or making an early spring picture under a large deciduous tree, or to furnish a slope or a steep bank which is difficult to mow, or masses of small bulbs and euphorbias in gravel, or just a mixture of decorative herbs. All these suggestions can create beautiful covering to any awkward place or difficult ground. Too large an area on the same level can become dull and uninteresting unless an occasional taller subject is introduced. Daphnes and tree paeonies could be used for this purpose in a sheltered spot or *Prunus laurocerasus* 'Otto Luyken', a low flowering evergreen laurel, a clipped box or even a large boulder in a more exposed one.

The idea of covering the ground with low beautiful plants can be put to many uses. Some people firmly believe that such a planting will keep down the weeds. That, of course, is a fallacy, but at least it leaves less room for the weed seedlings to flourish. One seldom gets the pattern right when making the first planting, but some of the

easiest which immediately come to mind must be lady's
mantle, pulmonaria, lamb's ear, campanulas and ajugas,
Ceratostigma griffithii, epimediums, hardy cyclamen and
ferns. Self-seeders like forget-me-nots, poached egg flower,
honesty, foxgloves and small bulbs are excellent and simple.
For trailing plants, possibilities include the double white
periwinkle *Vinca minor* 'Albo-plena', the variegated *Cotoneaster horizontalis* or *Cytisus* × *kewensis*. These would all
cover a large area. There are many plants which need a
damp place, such as kingcups, cuckoo flower, musk, primulas, ranunculus and hellebores – and all I have mentioned
are easily obtainable from friends or nurseries. There are
also forms of roses, clematis, vines, ivies and honeysuckles
that can be allowed to scramble over stones or a fallen tree
in a controlled manner. For 'glorious disarray', I allow
good plants to seed themselves and encourage them to

colonise by careful thinning. This is labour saving and, by the introduction of other plants among them, your man-made ground cover can become as near to a natural outcrop as possible.

I cannot begin to write fully on this very controversial subject in one short chapter. After all, Margery Fish took a whole book to tell us her ideas about ground cover. Her book *Ground Cover Plants* has recently been reprinted in paperback (Faber, 1980) and is full of good advice and suggestions. A garden is after all only a poor imitation of nature and if left to itself the ground would soon be covered with beauty whether we knew them as garden plants or as weeds. Often I have thought of my efforts of garden-making when in the Scottish highlands amongst the immense land-scapes of heather and gorse, or driving through miles of grey Mediterranean plants that make up the hot maquis in the plains of Portugal and Spain. It is when you come back after two or three weeks away that nothing, but nothing, can compare with that first slow walk among your own plants at home.

Cottage Garden Plants

I WONDER WHY one thinks of the cottage as always in a rural setting and thatched, with a white painted gate between hedges? Perhaps that is just yesterday's dream? Yet somehow, a cottage garden to most people does mean a flower-edged path to the door, beds under the windows, roses over the porch and a woodshed covered with clematis. And what could be better, for it is the absolute simplicity that makes the inviting picture. For the garden that is not going to get a lot of attention, a 'cottage' design with perennials and biennials could be the answer.

'Cottage' plants are really 'easy' plants that come up and flower year after year; and though it is most satisfying to know that they are there and will be popping up directly the spring comes, it is necessary to make sure that everything is left clear of weeds in the autumn. Most of the biennials are lovely and can be relied on to give a wonderful show each year if allowed to seed themselves: foxgloves, forget-me-nots, campanulas and sweet williams will cover the garden whether you want them or not. The self-seeding hellebores, particularly *H. corsicus*, make excellent border plants, and their leaves are decorative and evergreen; fennel, both green and purple, and angelica look right in such a garden, but they can be too prolific if not checked.

For height, tree poppies, *Romneya coulteri*, and hollyhocks look well; and they don't need staking which is a help. The sages make large colourful clumps and stay in good condition for several years. Both the purple-leaved and gold sages are particularly good, but the smaller variegated one needs a warm corner. Helichrysum, ballota, *Hebe* 'Pagei', all the lavenders, and rosemary mix well and are best planted closely to cover the ground.

For shrubs, use purple berberis and *Philadelphus coronarius* 'Aureus' with *Rhus cotinus*. They make a good foil for everything else and only need an occasional cutback in the autumn. In a cold or windy corner, use evergreen flowering shrubs such as laurustinus or any of the viburnums, with *Mahonia aquifolium* and the rugosa roses – and over and through them all, honeysuckle. In addition, choose the three-foot *Syringa velutina*: it is charming and scented and does not sucker as the others do.

Do not be carried away when planting bulbs, for they can

be difficult to manage and make the garden look rather too busy. But let there be golden daffodils to welcome you at Eastertide . . . and snowdrops by the seat under the fig tree.

Planting Old Garden Walls

ON A FINE DAY at the end of November, you wonder what you can do in your garden. It is too wet to get on the borders but, if not too cold, I always find something which needs doing to the wall plants and climbers. To keep old walls in good condition, they need continual attention; like the painting of the Forth Bridge, you just start again. Ivy is the worst hazard: one small piece of *Hedera helix* 'Goldheart' or *H. h.* 'Little Diamond' curling seductively up a pillar in the sunshine looks wonderful one day; but in a few weeks, the roots will be firmly embedded in old mortar and will soon loosen a flint or two. An east-facing surface of a wall is the most vulnerable because the morning sun drains the moisture from the mortar and so weakens the whole.

To grow a climber or a wall shrub, the wall should be wired, preferably at the time of building . . . but if the walls are like ours, the wires have probably rusted through and disintegrated! One of the main objectives is to see that no wind rocking occurs, for this can be fatal to tender young main stems. *Cytisus battandieri*, for instance, should have a stake to hold the main stem firmly – for they grow so quickly and often become weak or surface rooting. A wall looks at its best when well planted both for the winter and summer. I treat my walls as another dimension to the garden, following its overall design and ensuring they overflow with the differing colours and beauty of each season. The border which is to hold these plants and climbers must

be large enough to create a feeling of space and to give
enough elbow room for the clematis to fling its old man's
beard over the wall in the autumn.

A wall not only provides shelter from wind for plants,
but, together with the plants themselves, forms a microclimate in which so many tender things may not merely
survive but indeed make good growth and flower well.
Some of these rather special plants are *Berberidopsis corallina*;
the bold-leafed Mediterranean loquat *Eriobotrya japonica*;
Hebe hulkeana; *Tropaeolum speciosum*, the scarlet Scotch creep-
er, and *T. polyphyllum*, with grey leaves and tiny pale
orange-shaded flowers along prostrate stems; and three clematis: *C. armandii*, *C. rehderiana* (the cowslip-scented one) and

C. orientalis, which flowers until the frost. For several years, we have had such mild winters that it is all too easy to forget the heartbreak of '83, and, worst of all, '47 – for it is the freezing wind which is the killer. Plants like *Crinodendron hookerianum*, ceanothus, the hebes and daphnes, if they are staked against rocking and protected with straw or bracken or a forkful of cow dung over the roots, usually survive with their backs to the wall out of a continuous draught. It sounds a lot of trouble, but is well worth the effort – if only to know that having done what you can, they stand a chance of survival.

It takes many years to build up a collection of established shrubs and wall plants that are of true name and origin, or perhaps of one's own finding or crossing. Such a collection would be quite impossible to replace. The time spent on caring for the unusual and out-of-the-ordinary plants is never wasted. In fact, what makes the job of caring for wall plants so interesting is that few of them need the same attention!

Deep Shade

ONE WOULD NOT CHOOSE deep shade in which to make a garden – but there are many sites, especially in large towns, which are completely overshadowed and nothing can be done about it. To give any satisfaction, particularly in winter, I think the whole garden would need to rely for its beauty on design and dominating ornaments or other features, perhaps steps. Quite often, the trees are fully grown and beautiful – yet even at midday allow only filtered light through. It must be a daunting challenge to a would-be gardener, and I have often wondered what I would do in such a circumstance.

Much depends on the shape and size of the whole. Many such gardens are long and narrow, so it is not easy to create any element of surprise. If the dimensions are reasonable, I would first decide where I would walk, and to what. Secondly, I would consider what materials should be used for the paths, and the area I would need for planting or sitting.

As it would often be dampish in the shade, I should not choose any large stone slabs (such as York stone), on which one could easily slip, but a mixture of gravel and brick, using some larger paving to break it into interesting patterns – perhaps of blue slate or cobbles. You will find many ideas for paving in garden design books, but make sure you do not use the cobbles where you have to walk much because they are hard on the feet! Ashes also make a very acceptable path: they need to be well rolled and edged with bricks.

If possible, a garden should not be completely flat. Slopes increase the scope for planning as a whole concept – even if it takes years – and the garden then becomes one's own. Even a slight slope can be emphasized by steps, very wide and shallow, leaving space between the 'risers' for alpines in a mixed scree. The steps could lead to the very heart of your whole garden – and on the top step, a grand bronze? Or, more simply, a stone seat?

Timber arches or pergolas add interest but would not last long in damp shade unless very stout and strong. If the choice is stone, it should all be of the same colour and structure and will last for ever! You could use statues or some standing stones; one tall standing stone, at least seven feet high, and with a few *very* large rocks of the same kind of stone nearby, needs no flowers to enhance it; but hostas and hellebores complement all forms of stone or brick.

If you do create a solid garden picture that is satisfying, do not be tempted to use man-made containers or 'sinks' near it; rather, I think, small colonies of ferns with violets and primroses planted within a pattern of bricks and cobbles (more on these in the following chapters). It is important that this solid garden picture be built in scale with the whole, working from boundary to boundary using the complete length of the garden. Then from your door or French windows you walk immediately into your very own achievement. It will look well in rain or sunshine, summer or winter, though you will need a good broom to keep it tidy – there will be more sweeping than digging, especially if the trees are deciduous.

What can be grown in the shade before the trees come into full growth? *Prunus subhirtella* 'Autumnalis' flowers very early, and again in the autumn; *Viburnum plicatum* 'Mariesii' for its horizontal branches and good show of white flowers; the winter-flowering honeysuckle, *Lonicera standishii*, has very small white flowers on the bare branches in March, and another viburnum – *V.* × *bodnantense* – and, of course, the yellow winter jasmine. Some early bulbs –

scillas, snowflakes (leucojum) and *Erythronium dens-canis*, the dog-tooth violet, some low-growing very early species of tulips with variegated leaves, most of the alliums, the variegated *Arum pictum*, and perhaps a few miniature early daffodils. A small area of ferns, just among rocks, will stand out as a complete and distinct 'small garden' in itself; and near them, hardy cyclamen would make a quiet autumn picture and lily of the valley a charming spring one.

Violets

REALLY WELL-GROWN sweet violets can be very rewarding and this cultivated violet can be so good that, as a
gift, it is much appreciated by friends of any age. I was
given a Sussex trug basketful when I was ten by my god-
mother and their scent always reminds me of her and her
garden.

It used to be the hallmark of a good gardener to be able
to pick a bunch of well-grown sweet violets in January.
This large florist's violet has flowers at least half an inch
across, large dark leaves and a wonderful fragrance. Sweet
violets are seldom grown in gardens today and, unless
especially ordered, few florists keep them for sale. I am
surprised that they have not become fashionable again now
that so many people have become interested in plants. *Viola
odorata*, the old sweet long-stemmed violet, used to be
grown widely for market and was the pride and joy of all
good gardeners everywhere. Grown in frames, in a cold
house or in pots, it needs quite different culture from the
hardy ones. There are many named varieties. One of the
best is 'Marie Louise' which makes a fine strong plant, is
deep blue and has rather larger flowers than 'La France'.
'White Czar' has a lovely scent and responds well to liquid
feeding and a little warmth. 'Belle de Chatenay' is very
robust and full-flowering. We grew at home, and for market,
the 'Princess of Wales', which is one of the best for frame
work.

If the crop is to be successful at all stages of growth, the times and indeed the dates of taking and planting up the runners should be strictly kept. There are few comparable plants that need more attention to detail. Like sweet peas, the flowers need to be picked when ready, which may be best at the full bud stage. If a frame is used, it should be well built, deep and covered with glass lights which can be easily removed. The bottom of the frame should be of well-rotted manure and soil, topped up within ten inches of the lights when closed with an open gritty loam and compost mix. This must be done so that it has settled and is ready to be planted in early September and could well follow cucumbers or melons. The runners or crowns that you are now going to use were planted out in April, nine inches apart in rows twelve inches apart, under a wall or in a shady spot. They have been kept weeded and fed and any runners which have formed have been removed. In the second week of September, lift them and plant eighteen inches apart in the frame. They should be watered freely, daily in all but cold weather, and the lights should never be closed completely until it is particularly cold and frosty. Two blocks of wood placed between the light and the top of the frame can be adjusted to suit any outside temperature. The plant must never be allowed to dry at the roots and the whole frame should be kept damp but not wet. They need, therefore, shelter from frost and wind but must not be pampered, given plenty of air in warm weather and a weak liquid feed every three weeks. If very cold, put sacks or a covering of some sort over the lights, well pegged down, and remember that in a cold spell they need no water. Unless well arranged, frame culture can be very time consuming; but, with experience and organisation, the daily routine need take only a few minutes.

For growing in pots, plant a runner in a six-inch pot in April, stand out in the shade and water moderately. In May, sink the pots up to their necks in a frame and treat in the same way as those planted in the ground. Place them in a cold house on an airy shelf in early September. They must never be dry and always have plenty of air. They will respond well to a little warmth, but if too hot, they will become weak-necked and have pale flowers.

The main pests are slugs in the frame, green fly and red spider. Green fly can be controlled by giving more air and a gentle smoke; red spider means that they have been allowed to become too dry at some time, or too hot. Dust well with sulphur and water copiously.

There are other types of violet that are easy to grow and are hardy and vigorous. These grow well among other plants in patches of one colour – in a border where they have some shade in the summer. The American violet *Viola cucullata* with a mauve eye, and *V.* 'Swanley White' – also tinged with mauve – seed themselves readily and make acceptable tufts of green. They are lovely when massed, but have no scent. A good ground-covering violet is *V. reniformis*, scarcely two inches high with very small leaves and creeping stems. It is better to propagate it each autumn and plant again in May or June. There is also the small wood violet *V. sylvestris* which is white, and also comes in shades of blue, mauve and pink. Their true habitat is under a hedgerow or at the edge of a copse, for they cannot stand hot weather and need an airy spot. Other small ones of interest are *V. biflora*, which is yellow, the blue summer-flowering horned violet *V. cornuta*, and *V. gracilis*, which is violet-purple and a real gem from Olympia which will cover any well-drained soil. The Parma violet is double with a flat face, has lovely pale shades, but is more difficult to grow. There is also an old perpetual blooming variety named 'Saisons' or 'Violette des Quatres Saisons', which blooms through the autumn and winter with another burst of flowers in the spring. William Robinson talks of this and of the enormous plantations of it that were grown around Paris when he was a young man.

Double Primroses

GREAT FAVOURITES of mine, but difficult to grow, are the old double primroses. They need to be divided at least every three years, and some held in a frame to be safe from frost and slugs. I always thought the 'dividing' was one of the best jobs of the year: the roots smelled so delicious; but it was all very time consuming. To do justice to the double primrose, we can turn back to John Rees writing in *Flora* in 1665: 'The common double garden primrose is so well known that it is sufficient only to name it, but were it not so common in every countrywoman's garden, it would be more respected for indeed it is a sweet and dainty double flower of the chiefest of all English kinds.' In those days, there were many named varieties of this lovely plant: 'Madame Pompadour', 'Belvedere', 'Prince Silverwings', 'Quaker's Bonnet', and 'A Spring Darling' – to me, they sound like songs. There are the 'Bon Accord' polyantha primroses which were raised by the Cocker brothers at the beginning of the century in shades of blue, lavender and rosy purple, some flecked and shaded. William Robinson said in his classic *The English Flower Garden* (John Murray, 1892) that 'double primroses well grown and the same kinds barely existing, are such different objects that nobody will grudge them the trifling attention necessary to their perfect development'. And who knew better about good herbaceous plants?

An old primrose called 'Hose-in-hose' was described by

Gerrard as early as 1597 as 'double cowslips' and 'cowslips two in a hole having but one flower within another'. This primrose, then, is one in which one flower emerges from the centre of a second flower, giving it a duplex effect. In another, called 'Jack-in-the-green', the calyx forms a green leafy collar behind the flower and Parkinson called it 'franticke or foolish cowslip' and 'Jackanapes-on-horseback'. The Elizabethan gardener had a very limited choice of plants and therefore depended greatly on wild flowers. Double primroses flowered luxuriantly in these gardens of three hundred years ago in 'a mixture of rich loam and leaf-mould and a little shade'. They need to be mulched during the summer and watered well as they finish flowering and never allowed to dry out. I used to grow them in the heather garden among drifts of *Primula farinosa* and *P. forrestii*, and *P. × garryarde* 'Guinevere' whose dark leaves contrasted all the year with the pink flowers of the heathers.

Among the heathers, I grew large plantings of various *P. auricula* and always 'Queen Alexandra' – which is soft creamy pink and frilled. The old double primroses are not often seen today, but they should not be forgotten, for their flowers are beautiful and fragrant.

Interesting Paeonies

A BEAUTIFUL PLANT, and one which gives much satisfaction when grown well, is the genus *Paeonia*. The species are of very different growth and habit and all need a rich soil and wind shelter. When established, they should be left undisturbed and the moutans and tree paeonies should not be pruned unless absolutely necessary. *Paeonia officinalis*, the old cottage paeony, makes a strong plant and flowers for many years if mulched after flowering. The dark red one (*P. o.* 'Rubra Plena') is always in demand at Whitsuntide for church decoration and there is a pink (*P. o.* 'Rosea Plena') and a good white form (*P. o.* 'Alba Plena'). The herbaceous paeonies are very decorative and there are many varieties of single and double: they do much to enhance the mixed border but have very heavy flower heads and foliage which is easily damaged in rough weather. It is therefore better to stake them or control by wire or some other support early, before the flower heads develop. They will then look well in the border all summer. The supports will be completely covered by the plant's large decorative leaves (which turn a lovely soft pink in the autumn). The moutans (*P. moutan*) and the true tree paeonies are all hard-wooded and very beautiful. They grow to four feet or more and need a sheltered corner, for the flower heads and petals are very fragile. The moutans are of pale shades of yellow and lime and are early; but the tree paeonies are of many colours, both single and double.

Try and get them on their own roots, for the grafted ones often rot at the joint. I have grown them successfully from seed, particularly *P. mlokosewitschii*, *P. delavayi* and *P. lutea ludlowii*. They take more than a year to germinate and so should be sown as soon as they ripen in the autumn. They fill the pot with roots before showing any top growth, but after that can be handled with ease.

Why Not Try Something Different?

MANY PEOPLE TELL ME of their difficulty in finding plants that are 'different'. Garden centres tend to keep the species that everyone knows and so sell well. But good, unusual plants can be found and are well worth looking for. If you cannot find them yourself, grow them from seed.

Good seed is expensive, so buy from a reputable firm, choosing the varieties carefully. Take time to prepare your ground or boxes well. Follow the instructions and sow very thinly; then be sure they never dry out. Be adventurous and have fun, but do it well!

The soil is important, so use a suitable compost (which is easily available), or you can mix your own. You only need a few plants, so give them plenty of room to grow and transfer into small pots when large enough to handle. This degree of care is justified for special unusual plants: most perennials and herbs can be sown in a row in a nursery bed and planted out when and where you need them.

It is worth reiterating some good things which are worth raising and which I have mentioned earlier: hostas, primulas of all sorts, eucalyptus, lilies, especially *Lilium regale*, aquilegia, some named penstemons, violas, anchusa, *Salvia sclarea turkestanica* and *S. argentea*, and campanulas – especially *C.* × *burghaltii*. All can be sown in August or early September in short rows in a frame or cold house.

Try some small bulbs from seed sown where they are to flower. I have large patches of *Chionodoxa luciliae*, *Anemone blanda* and *A.* × *fulgens*, and many of the alliums, which have naturalized happily. Plants that you have raised from seed or cuttings and then established in your garden are really yours and are much more satisfying than anything you can buy.

Two rather special vegetables that are often difficult to find, but which can be easily grown from seed, are asparagus and sea kale. With a higher standard of marketing, good day-to-day vegetables are readily available so, again, why not try something different? Asparagus, when well established, grows well – but, like all crops, does need to be kept clean and well fed. Two- or three-year old crowns can be bought from specialist growers, but they are not cheap. I have had good results from seed, which should be sown in peat pots and planted out in June, care being taken not to damage the long soft roots. Place them on and over small heaps of soil in a well-prepared, free-draining oblong bed for easy cutting. Plant them in rows diagonally, twelve inches apart, and do

not cut the 'fern' until quite yellow – and then clear completely. An asparagus bed will last for many years and so
must be kept weed free. It is difficult to hoe because of the
soft roots, so a modern pre-emergence weedkiller should be
sprayed (as directed) before the growth starts in spring. Do
not cut at all in the first year, and in the second only
sparingly. All cutting should cease in early June.

Sea kale (*Crambe maritima*) is even easier. After all, it is
only a brassica! Plant out in July from peat pots, three feet
apart in clumps of four plants. Watch for slugs, and give
some shelter in the first winter. Cover the groups in January
with terracotta sea kale pots with lids – if you can find them
– they look so good! Cut the whole blanched growth when it
is about ten inches high, remove the pots, clean up and
manure well, covering again in January. The summer foliage
is delightful with large glaucous crinkled grey leaves – so
plant them where you can enjoy them, whether in a flower
border or by a purple decorative rhubarb.

Plant Hunting in China

I HAVE ALWAYS BEEN fascinated by the travels of plant hunters, particularly in China. I have lately been reading of the explorations of Farrer and Forrest and many dedicated men who faced much hardship and danger in their quest for plants. There has been the urge to care for living things since the necessity to cultivate crops for food and barter, but the greatest changes associated with agriculture and horticulture in this century must be associated with transport. In horticulture in my time, the extensive use of glasshouses for commercial crops has become a major industry, and in agriculture it needed two world wars to encourage the farmers to grow sufficient food for our needs. Transport was always a massive task: we have come a long way from the horse-drawn wagons. More incredible still, I think, was the transport by sea of plants from all over the world, first for medicinal purposes and later bringing trees, plants and bulbs for the botanic and physic gardens, and for the great gardens of Europe.

They came by sailing ship lashed in 'cases' to the decks or in dark airless holds below. Many ships were wrecked by storms or pirates and lives were lost with their cargoes of valuable plants. In 1564, Benlon, a doctor, collected around the Mediterranean, especially in Crete. He was followed by Cunningham in 1698 and d'Incarville in 1780. Some of their plants are still in cultivation: their survival for nearly 350 years seems impossible when you remember how easy it is to lose plants in your own garden!

People sometimes grumble to me about the names of plants and their length and difficulty of pronunciation. But it can be interesting to take them apart, word by word, and discover where they were found and by whom. When China closed her frontiers to all traders in 1750, Europeans, and particularly the British, were so abused by local officials that Lord Marcantey was sent to establish an embassy in Peking. Plant hunting was then only possible on a tour of official duty and any that reached Britain came via the diplomatic bag. Sir Joseph Banks was able to arrange for two 'botanic gardeners' to be in the embassy party, one of whom was Sir George Staunton, a Fellow of the Linnean and Royal Societies. The journey was difficult: a thousand mile trek overland and through the waterways of China in shallow-draught vessels to Peking. They reached Portsmouth a year later having had to keep clear of the French fleet on the way home, for we were by then at war with France. From that adventure, we now have only two plants: the Marcantey rose and a few camellias; much was collected but much lost.

The late Sir Frederick Stern of Highdown sponsored and encouraged the collection of some of the loveliest plants we grow: hostas, hellebores and tree paeonies. In 1842, after the opium war when Hong Kong was ceded to the British, Farrer was immediately sent there by the Horticultural Society and was home again in 1846 with eighteen cases 'filled with the most beautiful plants from North China'. Fortune, and before him, Kerr, were sponsored by Sir Joseph Banks and Sir Frederick Stern for about eight years. They found so many of the plants we all grow – or would like to: *Pittosporum tobira*, the Banksian rose, many begonias and lilies and the heavenly bamboo *Nandina domestica*. Their harvest also included much that is more familiar: camellias, azaleas, Japanese anemones, *Dicentra spectabilis* and the white wisteria, jasmine and forsythias. Later they were sent specifically to look for good varieties of tea plants with the East India Company.

In 1924, in his book *From China to Hkann Long*, Kingdom

Ward wrote: 'The plant collector's job is to discover the hidden beauties of the world so that others may share his joy. It is no unworthy aim to reveal what God has planted in the lost mountains since thereby may be revealed what He has hidden in the hearts of men.' What a great work they did for horticulture and how we should miss their discoveries! As I write, I can see from my window many shrubs and trees found in the wild in China and named after those early plantsmen. I think of their courage and endeavour – and it keeps my own gardening efforts in perspective!

A Retirement Garden

WHEN PEOPLE TALK of *a* garden or *the* garden or *their* garden, one knows by the intonation how much or how little it means to them – from joy to utter indifference. A garden can be one of remembrance, a scented garden, botanical, kitchen or winter garden; an allotment, large or small; just one's own patch. I meet many gardeners and age matters little: very young children – and it is usually small boys – will explain to me carefully what they grow and how. Some will tell me about the joy of a window box. It is important that a garden should be in no way belittled; young people especially need to do their 'own thing' and what better way than to try to grow something of beauty?

One particular – and interesting – kind of garden is for those who have retired. Two friends of mine have made a great success of their 'retirement garden': after some trials and error, they made a plan which they hoped would give them less work in the longer run and they have certainly achieved their aim. Not only have they satisfied their interests in plants, but they grow most of their own vegetables and salads and have a garden full of colour without too much hard work.

The whole garden is of grass and gravel; everything is grown either in the gravel or in greenhouses, pots or containers which are on the gravel or in the grass. There is a brick path the length of the house which leads on to a gravel area facing south: so it is dry and sunny and here, in

the gravel, is a profusion of flowers. Clumps of early daffs,
tulips, bluebells and scillas are followed by the purple and
golden sages, fennels and giant chives; then paeonies, iris,
and lady's mantle; there are also prostrate conifers. Among
these flowering plants are containers of every shape and size
filled with a rotation of flowering beauty: pansies, forget-
me-nots, wallflowers and later overflowing with summer geraniums, fuchsias, petunias, lobelia and penstemons. There
is a raised lily pool built up on brick and stone planted
around and down to the ground with campanulas, aubrieta
and sedums followed by summer plants and many annuals.
Behind the pool, in the gravel, are a few small shrubs for

early summer colour – a *Syringa velutina* and *Choisya ternata*; and, nearby, a wheelbarrow overflowing with bedding begonias and much more. The whole, though closely planted, is not cluttered: you can easily make your way through the containers to a greenhouse of red cedar and glass which is divided into two parts. The farther half is subdivided into three planting sections between which are flagstones which makes it easier to use the hose. In this farther half there are just vegetables: on one side are four or five potato plants and French beans followed by salads and perhaps a later sowing of beans. The middle section is of two varieties of tomatoes; on the other wall, cucumbers, peppers, a melon and boxes for raising seeds to plant in the containers or for growing on pot plants to take into the house. There is a dividing curtain which is drawn only for the first few weeks and then removed completely. The entrance half contains only flowers. It has a paved floor, two garden chairs opposite each other and a blind for use in very hot weather. There are hanging baskets, standard fuchsias, morning glory, ferns, two urns of begonias, lilies, fuchsias in pots, and against the wall, a geranium that reaches to the top of the house. What more could a retired gardener want?

But there is more! In the lawn, which is trim, edged and weed free, are trees and shrubs, well-grown and colourful and, as yet, not crowded. There is a twenty-foot-high *Eucalyptus gunnii*, a deep purple lilac, two spreading *Viburnum plicatum* 'Mariesii', a half-standard *Prunus* 'Pissardii', two golden conifers, a *Robinia pseudoacacia* 'Frisia' and one apple tree. Trained on the garden fence in the field are blackberries and near the greenhouse is a small frame of strawberries. There are runner beans on a frame against the garage wall near the back porch, with sweet peas between them and a smaller greenhouse. Here are more buckets and containers, this time planted with small vegetables: spring onions, broad beans, carrots, mint, sage and a rotation of new potatoes started in the greenhouse and brought out to ripen when in full flower. After the potatoes chrysanthemums are grown for the autumn and more salads along with wallflowers and sweet williams for the pots. The soil for these buckets of vegetables is most important: it has to be bought as compost and then mixed with what is necessary for each crop.

Although there is no real hard work, there is a lot of moving things about, and much that cannot be left to anybody else – especially the watering and the feeding. These two gardening friends of mine cannot leave for more than a day unless they have someone whom they can trust to water and feed, and possibly to tie in, pinch out, trim, disbud, thin or whatever. But everything – except the lawn mowing – can be done as and when they wish. It sounds exhausting, doesn't it? But to carry out such a programme one would be busy but not too busy. There is time to enjoy the bird song, to visit gardens and nurseries, time to sit and think; even time to just sit!

PART FOUR

TREES

Considering Trees

WHEN CONSIDERING TREES, my first thoughts are of beech woods and a carpet of bluebells, of dappled leaves over water and the soft colouring of the Sussex Downs. Trees are often thought of as a natural phenomenon and it is forgotten how important they are to the human and animal world and, aesthetically, how much pleasure they give to many people. The growth and habit of mature trees is so diverse that to know the names even of our indigenous ones, both in winter and summer foliage, can be most confusing. Since the middle of the last century, trees have been found in the wild and brought to the British Isles from all over the world and, because of our temperate climate, many of them do very well here.

Before planting around a homestead, or even just one tree in a small garden, their soil needs, resistance to wind, their eventual height and span of branches and tolerance of shade and interplanting must be given much thought; for when planting trees, one is looking twenty years on, and with hardwoods, much longer. Hopefully, one has time to watch their development, the winter colouring of bark and the different feel of trunks and main stems, some rough and deeply grooved and others as soft as silk. Many ancient trees assume a character of their own by developing gnarled formations around the base; others, especially limes and old apple trees, are hosts to the mistletoe.

Conifers, which were introduced here less than two hundred years ago, now dominate the skyline of our mountains and forests, much to the detriment, I think, of our native trees. In gardens, conifers of all shapes and heights can be useful and decorative and do provide stability in an otherwise deciduous planting; but there are some which outgrow their welcome if not carefully controlled and many should be completely removed before they overshadow the garden.

The crossing and intertwining of the branches of deciduous trees in winter, some upright and stiff and others thrusting through drooping or pendulous branches against an evening sky, make me feel glad that I had the inclination and encouragement to plant trees when we made the garden.

I realise how important it is that the older gardener should give positive encouragement to younger ones to plant worthwhile trees – even if it is to please others.

Planting Trees

TO HAVE THE SPACE, the discernment and the encouragement to plant trees as a heritage for one's great-grandchildren is a privilege for any gardener.

It is most important that a tree should be placed well – I say well in the sense of well-being to the whole, to give pleasure to those 'looking in' as much as those 'looking out'. A well-grown specimen, correctly placed, is not only important to the area, be it village, cathedral city or newly built estate, but is a joy to all, and if a joy, is less likely to be thoughtlessly cut down.

At Denmans we are now enjoying trees that were planted at the turn of the century: clumps and rows of evergreen oaks made a wonderful winter scene and windbreak. Older trees, the lime walk and eating chestnuts, planted about 1820 when the house was built, are getting rather battered, but the colour of their trunks is beautiful, deeply grooved and grey, like an elephant's trunk. The boles of those that have been felled are several yards round and eighteen inches high, forming hollows which hold rain water and fungi. A magnificent cedar of Lebanon towers above us all. Its branches have been chained together for at least fifty years but are well cared for and the tree still maintains its shape and condition.

A tulip tree, *Liriodendron tulipifera*, must have been an early planting on the estate. It stood in the park in 1946, a very sorry sight with broken and twisted branches. We could not save the tree but were able to have planks cut and seasoned, which in ten years made beautifully grained coffee tables of a bright amber colour. A liriodendron is majestic when in flower, but it often takes thirty or more years before this happens. We have planted two, the first is sixteen years old and last year (1988) bloomed well, as did many others in the south of England.

We started planting trees in 1948 but were not expecting to have so large a garden, so after putting in a *Thuja lobbii* windbreak and some *Chamaecyparis lawsoniana* 'Fletcheri' for stability, we did little planting for ten years. When I did start it was with winter-flowering shrubs and evergreens, and some small trees of interest. I thought even a magnolia too slow growing for me then, and now a *M. grandiflora* and a *M. stellata* have almost outgrown their allotted space.

It was about 1952 when I realised I must look ahead and plant more boldly. For longer-term beauty I planted a dawn redwood, *Metasequoia glyptostroboides*, and a maidenhair tree, *Ginkgo biloba*; a quince, medlar and walnut for their clear yellow and amber shades, so dramatic with dark leaves; some Japanese cherries; a parrotia and an *Arbutus unedo*. For quicker results I gambled with pittosporums and eucalyptus, and a *Pyrus salicifolia* 'Pendula'. Some of the best plantings that we have rely on evergreen shrubs for their satisfying shape, but the mixture must be well balanced. *Arbutus unedo* 'Rubra' takes many years to reach thirty feet and is not difficult to grow. It is beautiful in the early autumn when it fruits and flowers at the same time.

To place a shapely tree a long distance from the house, so that it becomes part of the backcloth to your daily scene, gives enormous pleasure. *Abies concolor*, the Colorado white spruce, is a superb evergreen for such a place; *Cupressus macrocarpa* 'Goldcrest' is a fast and easy grower and, seen from afar, is most attractive. The Camperdown elm makes a well-shaped weeping standard; its sweeping branches soon touch the ground so get as tall a standard as you can. It blooms on the bare branches, small reddish flowers like a parrotia, followed by greeny yellow seed heads. I had no fixed plan, I placed things that I liked with great care where I hoped they would form a backbone to the garden I hoped to make, and they did. After all, 'a man's reach should exceed his grasp, Or what's a heaven for?'

Shelter Belts in a New Garden

I SUGGEST YOU THINK first about the view, the prevailing wind and where you want to sit, and then have your soil tested. Your first impulse will be to clear everything up, but it is a pity, I think, to do this before you sit in the garden you are about to make, quietly by yourself, to get the feel of it. Plan your paths and where they will lead; plan your leisure space of grass or gravel near the house; and so, using your house as shelter, make the first planting of small trees and shrubs to continue that windbreak to give you a warm corner. Be sure that the garage and garden shed are accessible. If you are making your home in the country these need not be very grand but can make a beautiful addition to the house when covered with climbers.

There is nothing like a good hedge to make a sheltered garden; well cared for, it adds much to the homestead. Hornbeam, golden or variegated privet, yew, copper beech and laurel are all appropriate – but must be cut and trimmed once a year. Such a hedge, combined with a mixed shrub planting and grown as one concept, could be an ideal windbreak. It should be as deep as possible and the height and colour intermingled to give of its best on the garden side. Some grey-foliaged willow is valuable in the spring and the later berry and leaf colour makes a picture in the autumn. A few special trees arranged to stand alone – hopefully for your grandchildren – and planted far enough away from the house add a feeling of maturity to the surroundings. Eucalyptus, willow, viburnum, pyracantha, *Elaeagnus pungens* 'Dicksonii' and perhaps two golden conifers would make a stout buffer against wind and noise. In front of them, the garden border could have shrub roses, hebes and hydrangeas.

So now you have a windbreak and therefore a sheltered place for your breakfast or morning coffee. From that starting point, you can now work out what to dig and what to leave. Remember to curve the paths from the sitting area so that you can see right down and through the borders 'to something'. It need only be a silver birch or two and a seat, a sundial and flowers, lavender and herbs or just grass for the dog and the children; it could be a small special vegetable garden of salads, sea kale, asparagus, purple sprouting broccoli and calabrese.

Low interior hedges can form definite boundaries between different small gardens, enclosing perhaps a sundial or herb garden. They need only be a few feet high and could be rosemary, lavender or *Senecio greyi*. Roses make a wonderful flowering hedge about eight feet high – and as wide! – with hybrid musks, *Rosa* 'Felicia', R. 'Buff Beauty' and the R. *moyesii* seedlings.

You will, of course, be longing to get on with choosing your shrubs and plants and you will now know where you think you want to put them all. It is a good idea to keep a small weed-free piece of ground to hold the plants you are given or buy or bring with you until you have prepared your planting area, and you can sow the biennials and perennials you particularly like in rows in the same plot. The choice of material is so great that the result can be as simple or as elaborate as you care to make it, but don't be in a hurry to get it all done – let it be a joy to share with others for years.

A Dream Garden

A Glade of Trees

HAVE YOU EVER THOUGHT of planting just trees?
A glade of trees? A special dream garden that would be for
others as much as yourself? The clearance of so many
beautiful trees and woodland for new roads and building
projects makes it imperative that everyone, if they can,
should put back something towards the future landscape
whether for pleasure or commerce.

The site, therefore, would have to be carefully chosen –
for one's way of life, the soil and, of course, one's pocket.
The planting should be trees that may reach forty feet in less
than twenty years. My choice would be a sheltered half-acre
on the South Downs but a rocky coastal strip in Wester
Ross having the warmth of the Gulf Stream would suit me
quite as well thank you! – or a wooded valley on the Welsh
coast!

As my planting would need to be very selective, design
would be the first consideration; each tree when fully grown
would have been chosen for its position to enhance both the
garden and the whole district. There would be slender
shapely silhouettes, prostrate and compact undergrowth for
shelter, fastigiate and weeping specimens, all with the glories
of leaf, berry, stem and bark colour and of course fruit,
flower and scent in abundance. We should want it all,

133

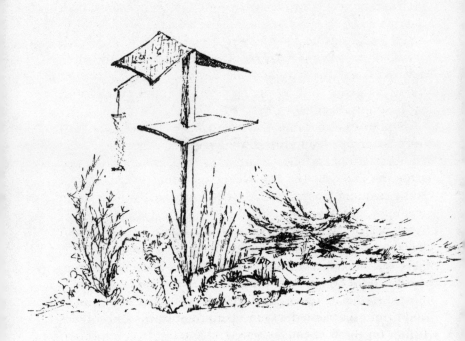

shouldn't we? It is an exciting thought that in these days of early retirement such a dream is a possibility and although it would take twenty years, one's days would be filled with something well worth while.

In this wild-wood type of garden there would be many difficulties with which to contend; there would certainly be rabbits, grey squirrels and mice and probably deer. The birds would be wonderful and your garden could be a real wildlife sanctuary, but unless one was a good shot and could control the vermin without disturbing the whole population it would be better to let nature do the controlling. I should do no digging other than the actual planting and be sure that a feeling of uncluttered space is accentuated by planning really wide rides, leaving a vista so that sunlight on the branches would create another picture. If the grass is too short there would be no wild flowers, so the last cut must be as late as possible so that their growth is not damaged, and the summer cut not done until after seed fall, and all the grass then raked up and off. The rides should be mown, I think, for it gives shape and a pleasant walking area. Perennial weeds are easily controlled with a spot gun and larger patches of brambles and so on by using SPK weedkiller and after the first year they would give little trouble.

It all sounds too simple, doesn't it? But if one looks carefully at well-managed woodland – there is your garden. You would need to plant groups of simple woodland plants which would eventually form a mass of colour every year – primroses, violets, fritillaries, woodruff, wild cranesbill, and cowslip, harebells and the early 'February Gold' daffodil. Wild white foxgloves and lords and ladies form good colonies and so do euphorbias and the green winter hellebore. More natural effects are created by colonisation than by ground cover. In about 1890 William Robinson – the author of *The English Flower Garden* – developed a wide range of perennials which he termed 'good garden plants' for colonising by self-seeding among meadow grasses, allowing them to compete with each other as in an alpine meadow. The white-stemmed *Rubus cockburnianus* against a dark holly or yew would create a striking effect: so would strong single roses growing up trees and through bushes, and red- and yellow-stemmed dogwoods with marsh marigolds in a damp spot.

My dream garden was to have been half an acre, but its size matters little. You might find a southern slope with a natural stream or your present garden is possibly quite as suitable. It is the design and planting that makes your dream come true.

Those Magnificent Evergreens

IT ALWAYS SURPRISES ME that more unusual
evergreen trees and wall shrubs are not generally planted.
So many ancient yews, box and holly have escaped the fury
of snow and wind for perhaps a hundred years and now face
the new menace of road-widening and the too-readily used
chainsaw. However, throughout Britain in old estates and
parks, there are still good stands of them along with the
near-indestructible evergreen oak. I have seen wonderful
evergreens planted for shelter and to clothe old castle walls
thirty feet high – and as wide: camellias, *Magnolia grandiflora*,
Phillyrea decora (*Osmanthus decora*), box and photinia all
growing together as one grand concept.

Our Victorian grandparents had much less choice than
we have. They planted extensively the cherry laurel, *Prunus
laurocerasus*; the Portugal laurel, *P. lusitanica*; and *P. laurocerasus* 'Rotundifolia', the hedging laurel, which gets so big
and ungainly that it is little use in our small modern gardens.
Nevertheless, some of the newer evergreens make good
windstoppers for tender plants. With erect racemes of
flowers, *P. laurocerasus* 'Otto Luyken' is outstanding: it is
dome-shaped, can be kept to a reasonable size, and flowers
well. Two other interesting laurels are *P. laurocerasus*
'Marbled White', broadly conical with grey-green and white
leaf variation; and *P. lusitanica* 'Myrtifolia', with small leaves,
which is a good substitute for *Laurus nobilis*, the bay tree, in
cold areas. Box, yew and bay were used for topiary work in

tubs for the lawn or conservatory and were also allowed to grow into large rounded banks for shelter. Thick yew hedges often succumb to red spider infestation which gets right into the tinder-dry wood and is very difficult to reach in the centre of an old hedge. It is possible to control the spider by wetting the infected wood and then spraying with Malathion as directed, for red spider cannot abide wet conditions.

On and around old stables and cobbled yards, and hugging the walls of ruined buildings and churches, one often sees plants which would be difficult to find in even a good garden centre. Not often seen are *Trachelospermum jasminoides*, *Clematis armandii* and *C. cirrhosa balearica*, *Distyleum racemosum* or even *Garrya elliptica* or *Coronilla glauca* – yet all only need wind shelter and are evergreen. Some good evergreen scented shrubs which will stand on their own or in a planting, and that nearly everyone can grow, are sarcococca, *Choisya ternata*, most of the daphnes, *Pittosporum tobira*, the skimmias, mahonias and *Osmanthus delavayi*. (For more information on their flowering, see the next section.)

For lower evergreens to clothe the ground in winter, try some tufted spreading perennials such as the green hellebore, thrift and bergenia, rock roses, lavender and rosemary.

I have not mentioned any of the beautiful variegated evergreen trees and shrubs which add so much beauty to the winter garden. The variegated silver or gold-edged ivies should not be forgotten: they make excellent ground cover if controlled; nor should the stout elaeagnus in all its forms – it even stands up to salt spray. Bamboos of differing heights make a dense and emphatic background which can be very useful in a large garden.

With so much that can be grown in our temperate conditions, it is often difficult to decide what are the most appropriate plants to form a natural mix. Many people think first of conifers when thinking of evergreens; but they should be used very sparingly for they are mostly foreign to Britain and unless correctly placed soon outgrow their position and look incongruous. I remember being told how out-of-place the Scots pine looked when first introduced to our rolling Sussex downs, and the tale was that the locals pulled up as many as they dared when out walking. Trees that are not of a district so rarely look right in the wild. The three main ways to use them are for ground cover, for sheer bulk and for a silhouette on the skyline. An ideal way to assess their use is to study them from as far away as possible and in winter as well as summer. Conifers make such an impact on gardens – and indeed the district – that it is necessary to choose each for its special place; and to be sure of correct naming it should be bought from a specialist conifer nursery.

Oh! to be in England
now that April's here

AND WITH APOLOGIES to Robert Browning, I add
that I am always glad to be in England, especially in May
and June when so many of our decorative trees and shrubs
are at their best. The countryside is so beautiful at that time
of the year and our gardens so full that it is difficult to make
a choice if one is looking for a plant suitable for a particular
spot.

When looking for an appropriate tree or shrub, much
depends on the soil and how sheltered you are from cold
winds. As I've said, it is as well to grow only those plants
which like your soil, but near-neutral soil, regularly enriched
with farm or garden compost, will grow nearly anything
you wish. Having decided to replan part or even the whole of
your garden or plantation, or perhaps just to introduce
something different to your own design, I suggest that you
should think first of those small deciduous flowering trees
that will give colour, and sometimes scent, for at least part
of those wonderful months.

The town garden should not be overshadowed; but in the
country, some height can be achieved by planting trees in
the boundary hedge, forming a windbreak. These possibilities should be considered well before making your final
decision and though that is always a personal one, I will
suggest some small trees that I have grown and found
good.

Stachyurus praecox and *Corylopsis spicata* usually flower in

March and so make a good starting point. *Magnolia stellata* will slowly make a ten-foot many-branched shrub and is covered with small white flowers in early April. The viburnums are extremely hardy and make acceptable shrubs and small trees. They give a grand display of flowers and scent in April and the whole bush will mix well with others until leaf fall. *Viburnum carlesii* is an old one but has more scent than most of the others and the leaves turn a soft pink. *V. plicatum* 'Mariesii' flowers along its horizontal branches and three together will create a splendid planting in grass. Camellias are grand evergreens, their dark leaves making a perfect foil for summer plantings, and as they start flowering in March and early April they should face west to escape the morning sun on their wet or possibly even frosted petals. I would always choose *Magnolia grandiflora*, which takes many years to grow too large and can, with care, be cut. It has large cream chalice-like flowers with a distinctive boss of stamens and a spicy fragrance of lemon. *Osmanthus delavayi* grows slowly to five feet and as wide, and has small white flowers in early April.

It is easy to find good flowering shrubs that reach four or five feet to flower in May or June. They form the substance of most well-planted gardens. Here are a few particularly worth mentioning: *Choisya ternata*, *Pittosporum tobira*, sarcococca (which will be nearly over by April, but which has good leaves), *Euonymus radicans* and *E. japonicus*, both gold and silver leaved. Daphnes make shapely bushes with beautiful and very fragrant flowers. They have the reputation of being difficult, but if fed with compost and planted in good rich soil, usually do well. The easiest evergreens are *Daphne odora* and *D. odora* 'Aureomarginata' together with *D. collina* which makes a big round bush and flowers for months. *D. laureola* has yellow flowers and strong pointed foliage; it has a dwarf form, *D. l. phillipi*, barely six inches high, *D. blagayana* is prostrate, but requires a stone or two to keep it so. The semi-evergreen *D. × burkwoodii* 'Somerset' makes a two-foot bush and is very sweetly scented.

Fatsia japonica is a good evergreen which will grow to five or six feet or more if allowed; it has good leaves all the year round and spectacular flowers in October. The false heath fabiana is a reliable border plant and *Erica arborea*, the tree heath, will grow to eight feet if sheltered. *Photinia serrulata* 'Red Robin' has scarlet young foliage like the pieris but does not need acid soil; *Itea ilicifolia* has racemes of greenish-white drooping catkins in late summer and is a cheerful bush all year; and, of course, don't forget the hard-wearing *Senecio* family. For height, eucalyptus is good and it can be cut for decoration and so kept at the height you wish. The half-hardy Mediterranean sub-shrubs are many and various: rosemary, lavender, the hebes, ballota, sun roses and ozothamnus are all indispensable, but they do like to be out of the cold wind.

A collection of trees and shrubs alone does not make a garden. Your design or setting may be borders or large plantings within gravel or grass, or you may be lucky enough to have a wall which always makes a perfect background. But all should be carefully considered before you start to plant. I like to use half-standard flowering trees in the border among other shrubs and herbaceous plants, for they make homes for shade lovers and give height. It doesn't matter whether your garden is small or large if, by getting the mixture right, your final planting gives you pleasure.

Replanting Our Garden Trees

I SUPPOSE THERE HAS never been the incentive to plant trees on such a scale in southern England as there is now in the aftermath of the great gale. This generation has a wonderful opportunity to plant the right trees in the right places; and everyone can obtain professional advice – and in some cases help – even if planning to plant only a few trees or to fill in gaps in the hedgerows. The trees you plant are important to us all and to our children. Thankfully, there are already signs of much good planting in Sussex.

As gardeners, let us make our contribution to the project by replacing any small flowering garden trees we have lost, or at least some of them, and let us take the trouble to plant them well. People are often saddened by their gardens being overshadowed by large trees which they cannot, or must not, remove. Certainly trees should not be felled without good reason, but a conifer which has outgrown its position and beauty becomes a dangerous and space-consuming hulk and is not a pretty sight. Unfortunately, the trend of gardeners today is toward haste and instant gardening has become a habit. A small garden needs small decorative trees and there are many that are beautiful, both in leaf and fruit, which will not outgrow their allotted space and which will give pleasure for a long time. The trees you plant are your choice, but much depends on the soil, of course, and, indeed, on what your neighbour has already planted. Ideally,

you may add your boundary trees to theirs and so form a wind shelter for both gardens.

Evergreen trees take a lot of planting space, so possibly deciduous ones such as silver birches, sorbus or maples would allow you more room beneath them for a spring garden or bulbs. When planting for privacy, use large evergreen shrubs which can be kept to any size you wish by the careful cutting out of unwanted wood. Three decorative small trees with gold foliage which are good for lighting up dark corners are *Robinia pseudoacacia* 'Frisia', *Catalpa bignonioides* 'Aurea' and the golden-leaved elder, *Sambucus nigra* 'Aurea'. For silver foliage, *Pyrus salicifolia* 'Pendula' is a beautiful small weeping tree, *Pittosporum* 'Garnettii' needs a fairly sheltered position, and *Eucalyptus gunnii* is lovely in later summer (and if cut every year, will then keep its fine juvenile foliage). Small purple trees are not so plentiful but a half-standard *Prunus* 'Pissardii' or a half-standard *Acer platanoides* 'Crimson King' make good small trees for shade; another, reaching only ten to twelve feet in height, is the purple nut *Corylus maxima* 'Purpurea' which is a lovely shade of purple. For those with larger gardens, there is a far wider choice: *Parrotia persica* is graceful and has interesting foliage all the year round with good autumn colour; liquidambar makes a large tree with five-lobed maple-like leaves with autumn tints of crimson and purple (but not on chalk!); and a large white cherry is a 'must'.

The years following the gale of '87 could be our chance, and maybe our duty, to replace some of the wealth lost to us, not only in the storm, but also in the building of houses and roads and other modern-day needs that swallow up so much productive land. Many of our hedges have been cleared to make it easier to use modern machinery more effectively, but the countryside looks more beautiful with the young trees growing where they are seeded in the hedgerows. Yet we tend to take our roadside trees as a right; forgetting that someone had to plant them – or, when hedge-laying and trimming, that someone had the sense to let the young saplings grow on. It is a matter of great concern that seldom, or never, will this land give again as much wealth of food and timber. It is a fact that we must all accept, but in these days of plenty our prayer should be that future generations will not need that wealth.

PART FIVE

MONTHS AND SEASONS

January

Tool-shed Reminiscences

IT IS A LITTLE TOO EARLY in the year to enjoy most jobs in the garden, except possibly a brisk hour digging in the vegetable patch or having a good bonfire. However, if you want to get outdoors and the weather is reasonable, there is always something which needs attention, even if it's only in the tool shed. With the new year stretching before us, there seems plenty of time to carry out all those plans thought out while going through the catalogues – but somehow, the gardener never catches up (and usually blames the weather!). The tool shed, however, may have its exciting moments: those long-lost secateurs found at the bottom of a box of dead and dried-up myrtle. . . . For what vase or bunch of flowers were those picked, I wonder, as I wade through more boxes, most of which are too broken for anything but kindling use. Hanging on the wall is an old wooden dibber, rotten with worm and age, but I can just see the letters burnt into the handle: R D, and under that, something C, and then the J H R that I added thirty years later.

Time means little when making and planning a garden. Old tools have a character of their own: a wooden hayrake, or what is left of it, and a long-handled dung fork bring back memories of hard work. Perhaps it is as well that a tool shed should not be too tidy, for memories can be sweet as

well as sad. Outside, standing against the wall, are two properly inscribed tombstones dated August 10th 1908 and 'at the end of the nineteenth century at Westergate House'. They are in memory of dogs named Smut, Pepper, Myrtle, Jock and Scamp, 'faithful friends and companions of the Denman and Millbanke family'. How true it is that homesteads and gardens are not made solely for a known time: hedges of laurel and box, and ancient apple and pear trees, if not pruned too heavily, have been known to grow well and to bear fruit for a hundred years or more.

Of course there are other things to do in January besides reminiscing in the tool shed. In the garden, you may find *Iris stylosa* and the mottled leaves of *Arum pictum* and winter jasmine, which looks so well when arranged in an old mug with the small pointed leaves of *Hedera helix* 'Little White Diamond'. The mahonias, especially *M.* × 'Charity' are for November and December, but the long catkins of *Garrya elliptica* will open and lengthen in a warm room.

Many biennials may come and go for generations in an old garden if the texture of the soil has not been damaged.

We have *Campanula pyramidalis*, the chimney bellflower, which appears year after year in the most unlikely places – often on the top of old walls, and last year a large plant appeared in the gravel close to the front door! They used to be grown here at Denmans as pot plants for house decoration and I remember seeing rows of them standing by the conservatory wall in 1926 and, though I have never sown any seed, they are still with us.

Hand-made clay pots and the larger sea kale and rhubarb pots with lids are things of great beauty. Many have thumb marks around the lip where they have been turned on the wheel; sometimes they have the initials or name of the maker; and, occasionally, that of the pottery. The tools of the farmers and gardeners in those days were of necessity strong and well made, of different seasoned woods chosen for their particular job. When we came to Denmans in 1946, we found a box of small wooden wedges and wooden turnbuttons for the greenhouse windows and larger wooden wedges and blocks for the frames. On a shelf in the conservatory was a small wooden hammer, lightly made with a handle barely six inches long for the head gardener's sole use to check, by tapping the pots, the correct watering of the plants.

The BBC television series *The Victorian Kitchen Garden* showed so well many of the old tools and their uses and reminded me of what we did and how it was done. I'm sure gardeners today would miss their rubber boots and light-weight clothing if they were to work in such conditions, and many would find it difficult to grow such wonderful crops – even having resource to more than just composted animal and vegetable materials.

The pleasures of reminiscence! . . . But back to work!

February

Getting Started

IT'S THAT FEBRUARY FEELING, that moment of doubt between Christmas and the spring when you think of those small bowls of violets and wintersweet; and, having exhausted all the bulb catalogues and read and re-read the plant lists, you wonder if you are sure you want a garden – or whether you are simply feeling that you must keep the place tidy. You dare not allow yourself to think of the summer and the exciting things you could grow – for that would be the beginning of the end. Could you make a garden? Have you the time? An awful anticipation of failure haunts you. Where could you start? When? Your friends tell you that all it needs is half a day a week, or half an hour a day – just to keep fit. But you are fit and you have not got half an hour to spare. You have a fear that once started, it will never be finished. And you are right: it never never will be finished. Then you think that it would be nice for the children; you remember relaxing round a friend's patio and barbecue. Perhaps you should start!

Once you have started on your own patch, that is that. You will think of little but design and colour, paths and plants. You will soon have exhausted all the library can lend you and you will have had your soil tested. Meanwhile, your family keeps rather aloof and wonders if you should take a break. But it remains a fact that many people find gardening a satisfactory, if time-consuming, hobby; and that working with colour and design fulfils an artistic sense they did not know they had.

It is sometimes called 'working with nature' – but more often it works the other way. You are surprised to find that you listen more carefully to the weather forecast; late frosts, winds and drought concern you. Your plants are attacked by cats, moles and birds and you have green fly, blackspot and backache. You ask yourself: 'Is it worth it?' My own answer, after sixty years of joy and frustration is: 'Yes, certainly. Yes!' Rudyard Kipling's consolation is that 'when your back stops aching and your hands begin to harden, You will find yourself a partner in the Glory of the Garden'.

We always think of February as a dark damp month, but as the days get longer and the birds busier comes the urge to get out and about. But do not be tempted to start on the borders or you will do much damage to the texture of the soil. Early snowdrops and the red winter leaves of bergenia in front of evergreens or a wall make a lovely display in the winter sunshine. Everything starts in February: the early bulbs, violets, primroses; the hedges show just a tinge of green, and, of course, the grass needs cutting and the peaches spraying against leaf curl. There are seeds to sow and half-hardy plants to pot on, so you can't really leave your garden for long. Looking forward into the new year gives a feeling of elation – and perhaps also some fear of what the forces of nature have in store for us!

There is, of course, always something one ought to be doing. Rhubarb should be covered if you want those tender pink shoots. The asparagus bed will need to be hand weeded, left level and raked for the special pre-emergent weedkiller that should be sprayed over the entire clean bed, well before the spears come through. At least four hours of fine weather is needed after spraying, and the soil thereafter should not be disturbed at all and then you will have few weeds, if any, all the season.

Out and About

THERE IS ALSO that other February of the fields and the woods, so why not forget about your plans for a while and discover it. There is nothing like the great, silent outdoors to blow away the winter cobwebs and while the leaves are off the trees, there will be better views. I do not mean that you should start this tomorrow, whatever the weather, because as much fun can be had from plotting your route as from the trip itself.

Here in Sussex, we have the Downs and the sea, and both are accessible. It is possible to walk all day on the Downs and see no one, and yet to see a variety of terrain. There are deep woodlands and open down, chalk streams and ancient bridges – all within a ten-mile walk, although in February, it is likely that our tidal River Arun will be fast flowing and often flooded.

To walk along the ridge of the South Downs is a great experience. There are bridle paths, well signposted all the way and the views are spectacular: northwards across the Weald and southwards over the coastal plain (with glimpses of the sea and the coastline). It is possible to arrange for bed and breakfast, or even to put up a tent (though not in February!), if by good planning you have managed to arrive at a suitable place. This walk cannot be hurried, so you should choose a quiet clear day or two, midweek if possible, and there are four things you can't do without: a camera, a compass, a good map and binoculars.

In damp woods under the overhanging branches of mature trees there is so much to see and hear. In the late afternoon, there are hundreds – no, thousands – of birds and small animals preparing to settle for the night; and strangely, some of them make a lot of noise about it, particularly the pheasants and blackbirds! Most small birds quietly find their sheltered nooks, but the wren makes a great fuss as she finally settles; the rabbits, having a last nibble, don't go far from their warrens; the deer are very sensitive and take a long time to approach their snug hiding places among the bracken and the gorse. A twig snapping underfoot will start the pheasants' warning squawk. You must stay quite still until it is dark, to enjoy that feeling of utter silence to the full.

I have also enjoyed walking in Greece, Portugal and the Spanish Alps, plant hunting with friends. This has enabled me to go further and higher than I could have done alone. I enjoyed the softness of Greece and the mountain flowers, but I am glad not to have missed walking in Snowdonia, the Dales and in the Western Isles, watching the golden eagles in the mountains of Skye and sea birds along that coast. There are beautiful gardens to see in Scotland and in the north, and in Wester Ross the Gulf Stream has made possible the exotic gardens of Inverewe, where there are many plants one would not expect to see in Europe except around the Mediterranean. It is so simple nowadays to fly to a warmer spot than ours, but if you are prepared for the weather that makes our British countryside so green and beautiful, you can have no greater pleasure than walking in the hills at home – and your garden will still be there when you get back.

March

Early Arrangements from the Garden

IT IS DURING the short days early in the year that one most appreciates the first flower arrangements. It is delightful to pick a large double-handful of snowdrops – the early and the late varieties come out in a rush if there have not been hard frosts – put them in a two-handled mug deep enough to take the long stems; arranged with leaves of *Arum italicum* and those of cyclamen, they look lovely. I pick *Iris stylosa* whose open flowers smell so sweetly of that spicy fragrance that is peculiar to all irises; they should be plucked in tight bud since they last so short a time. The cream and white polyanthus have been in bloom all the winter under the nut trees together with the semi-wild violets of white, pale pink and mauve. These are so small when they first arrive that I can smell them before I see them – but later I put them into an egg cup with a few pointed leaves of the variegated ivy, making a delightful miniature arrangement. The early pale mauve *Crocus tomasinianus* seeds itself among the aconites in the gravel under my window and they show up well against the dark-leaved hellebores: the Lenten roses, *Helleborus orientalis*, are now fully open – too early if we have many March winds. They pollinate easily, so we have many soft colours, pink through to deep purple, but to keep a good strain we need to ensure that only the best colours are kept. *H. corsicus* will also lose its vigour and depth of colour unless only the better ones are left to seed. *Cornus mas* is flowering well and also *Parrotia persica*, with small red tufts of blossom on the bare stems. The most elegant of the early spring flowering trees must be, I think, *Stachyurus praecox*, which has creamy-yellow catkins followed by plum-coloured foliage and perfectly complements the nearby camellias. There is so much beauty, but so much to come: the scillas, chionodoxas, alliums, jonquils, narcissi, daffodils and tulips, large and small, will all make a grand display before the rush of spring really starts.

Most people put spring first in their choice of seasons, but for me it must be late May, June and July when there is absolutely no soil showing in the flower borders at all. Always in March, there is a chance of wintry wind and rain, but we can still dream of further planting and of fresh fields to conquer. And by putting the right plants together in well-chosen positions your garden may be beautiful in any season.

Spring in the Air

I WAS ONCE ASKED by a small boy: 'Does spring come after winter or before summer?' My answer was not as explanatory as I would have liked. Spring in the woods certainly comes after winter: under the leafless beech trees, after a long wait for the warmth of a few sunny days, the bluebells and the violets thrust themselves up through the dead leaves. Through the March winds and the 'blackthorn winter' – that spell of cold weather which usually occurs when the blackthorn is in flower at the end of April – the growth on the hedges seems at a standstill. But come a few April showers and everything is out at once, spring is nearly over. . . . It is all so fleeting.

Spring on farmland that has been well cultivated just rushes along: grass, weeds and spring corn all seem to grow inches in a night and the fields look wonderful, rolled and neat in the sunshine. All winter work is at an end and there is no time now to mend that roof: spring on the farm seems to come not only before, but into, summer.

When spring comes in the garden, you try to get the best of both worlds: if you have planted small early bulbs near the house, under the shelter of an evergreen shrub, you have made a start. Many people think that bulbs, if scattered in grass, are easy and labour saving; however, even if planted in groups they can double the work of the man with the mower.

Spring in the garden is so personal, especially near the

house: the odd plant you have been given or bought has been popped in until you can deal with it. Suddenly, it is in bloom among the herbs at the back door. All at once you have everything: flowers, weeds and slugs. It is a busy life, for now you must sow the flower seeds; and the vegetable garden needs attention. But by the time the cuckoo is calling, all will be done, and you will wonder why you ever thought it wouldn't be.

And after April, when May follows

*'And after April, when May follows,
And the whitethroat builds, and all the swallows!'*

GARDENERS ARE ALSO BUSY, for everything grows so fast in May, especially the weeds. The cherries and magnolias are in bloom and the lilacs, clematis and fruit trees are bursting. It would be nice to have breakfast out of doors and to sit and admire it all, but there is much to be done!

Apart from cutting the lawns, keeping things trim and tidy and putting out your summer plants, the kitchen garden will now need attention. By gently hoeing through your vegetable patch in May before the weeds take over, a fine tilth can be formed in the top inch of soil which helps to keep the ground from dying out. As you do this, the shallots and spring cabbage that you planted in October can well do with a mulch of garden compost or manure and the early potatoes that you put in on Good Friday will need earthing up. The spring onions and onion sets should be looking good and the row of early peas should be guarded in some way from birds. Runner and French beans can now be sown and the ground prepared for the small vegetable seeds: carrots, beetroot, spinach, parsnip, leeks and most of the brassicas, thinly in rows, and, of course, lettuce. It is a good idea to sow a pinch of different sorts of lettuce and radish seed together every ten days to keep a succession of salads going. Sweetcorn, sweet peas, runner and French beans, which were sown five in a pot in March in the greenhouse, can be put out after May 11th – that being the date after which there are traditionally no more frosts! Sweetcorn should be planted out in blocks, not rows, for better pollination and the sweet peas planted in good rich soil with their growing points pinched out, leaving only one or two pairs of leaves to encourage root growth. Outdoor tomatoes should be potted on and, if ready, cucumbers and melons moved into small pots in the greenhouse. (A second sowing of tomatoes is advised in April.)

May is the only month in which it is possible satisfactorily to divide water lilies and pond plants and to clear unwanted weed – but always leaving enough to shade the water. If sea kale pots are now removed, the root stock can make good summer growth ready to cover again in January. And the asparagus must be kept free of annual weeds.

So May is a busy month, one of great beauty with many soft shades of green and amber as the leaves of the acers and sorbus unfold.

Pale Buds of May

HOWEVER, MAY CAN also be a treacherous month: despite tradition, there is always the dread of late frosts. A keen gardener is never far from those tender plants he cared for all the winter. So do not be in a hurry to put out your half-hardy plants from boxes or pots: they seldom make good if once checked by a cold night. It is better to hold them in a wheelbarrow under a north wall where they can be kept moist, but not too wet, for a day or two. I attempt to grow and hold in the cold house or frame those things that give the garden a little bit extra later on. Some of the salvias are good for this: *S. sclarea turkestanica*, *S. involucrata* and *S. argentea*, the species *Tropaeolum* and some of the less hardy Mediterranean grey plants, ballota, *Carex morrowii*, fuchsias, penstemons, and tovara with its variegated leaves. If you have room, plant in threes or fives and next to some colourful leaves so that they may complement each other and make a picture to last all the summer. There are many pale annuals that can be grown from seed in boxes and planted out – or sown later *in situ* – in the places you have left.

This is a time when you often need to water; in my garden, under the old walls, the ground can get very dry and hot for shrubs and climbers, even in May. It is a good idea to put a large flat stone or a forkful of manure or compost over the roots of a clematis, for they like their feet cool and their heads in the sun. Perennials in the borders look splendid after a lot

of rain, though they are rather too forward. The heraldic
thistle, angelica, the fennels and verbascums have made a lot
of leaf; and one of the joys of May are the euphorbias –
though they do spread rather they can be controlled, as can
the alliums. And we could not do without the golden thyme
and the variegated sages and apple mint.

Try mixing the pale yellow *Daphne pontica* and Bowles'
golden grass with *Rhus cotinus* and a purple berberis: they go
well together. Pale colours, particularly lime and not yellow,

as I recommended earlier, show up so well at this time of year in the borders and shrubberies. They can light up the whole garden, giving weeks of interest before the strong colours of June and July take the stage. For trees and shrubs, I suggest *Robinia pseudoacacia* 'Frisia', *Sambucus nigra* 'Aurea', *Euonymus radicans*, especially 'Emerald 'n' Gold'; and most of all, the gold-leaved *Philadelphus coronarius* 'Aureus'. So many growing things have such a short term of beauty: often within a day they are damaged by wind, slugs or frost – or just badly placed – and it is easy to forget how perfect they can be.

The very young leaves of a red oak are pure amber. They have no other colour or shade at all, and as the long pointed buds of a tree paeony open, one wonders at their beauty. But other things follow so quickly, they are almost forgotten. When, after a wet spring, everything bursts into flower fast one has to be careful not to miss plants at their best. I shall be sorry when the elms and the beech trees have dropped their small green circular flower sheaths, and the poplar *Populus candicans* their long catkins.

One of the greatest pleasures of May in the wild are the beech woods with their pale-green drooping branches over a carpet of bluebells and anemones. Roses, of course, are for June, but if the weather is good there is one outstanding yellow climber that flowers in May: the Banksian rose. But it likes a well-sheltered wall and is best not pruned except to control its growth after flowering. Some easy but beautiful May perennials with delicate foliage make a perfect little woodland garden under the pale leaves of the Himalayan whitebeam or *Acer platanoides* 'Crimson King'. At the moment, mine has Solomon's Seal, three different varieties of alliums, the handsome variegated arum leaves, the crinkled leaves of lady's mantle and the black ones of *Viola labradorica*. The seed heads and star-like pointed leaves of the green hellebore, bluebells and, on the path edge, ajuga and golden marjoram together make a wonderful woodland planting.

Glorious June

BEING AWAKENED by blackbirds and the persistent call of the cuckoo can demand breakfast in the garden. In light summer clothes and under a cloudless sky, a few chores and shopping can be a pleasure. Then, with a crisp lettuce from the frame and a long cool drink in one's hand, it is possible to settle for a sleepy hour in the garden. I wonder lazily what I should do with the afternoon, but an early cup of tea in the shade seems to be the answer – where one can admire the borders which are now ablaze with colour. Obviously there is no time today to start any serious gardening, so to the sound of tennis balls plopping in the distance and chattering children on their ponies trotting down the lane, you allow yourself slowly to fill a basket of weeds.

Summer has arrived and that first day, in shirtsleeves with windows and doors wide open, your home and garden mean something very good indeed. Our green and pleasant English gardens, lush meadows and well-tilled farmland all result from our much-maligned weather! Is anything more discussed or disparaged, I wonder? It is, of course, an important subject. As people go about their work and play, indoors or out, in town or country, the absorbing topic of conversation is the weather.

It is essential to the grower of outdoor crops that the seed bed should be prepared correctly – and, weatherwise, this operation is often the most hazardous. But apart from those who earn their living on the land, there are gardeners who battle on through drought or cloudburst. During a prolonged drought, standing hose in hand considering which plants to water and which to leave to fate, it is a humbling moment when that first drop of rain falls. Those who deal with growing things know well that rain does more good than any sprinkler, but whatever the weather, June is the time of flowers, and especially roses. Long summer evenings filled with their scent and the sound of bees are what we all expect of this glorious month.

Roses are most accommodating, for they fill so many needs. A well-chosen variety for a particular spot will flower for years if allowed to do what it wants to do, perhaps to ramble over a garden shed or trained up over an old wall. There are some strong-growing spectacular ones, which need an old apple tree or some large expanse to look their best. R. *filipes* 'Kiftsgate' is one, R. 'Mermaid' and R. 'Wedding Day' are also just as suitable and need little attention except for the cutting out of dead wood and the tying in of strong young growths. There are so many new roses now that I find it impossible to get to know all of them and their needs, and I am glad that some of the best of the old ones are still in demand and available.

A Warm Summer Evening

TO GROW WELL is not necessarily to garden well. To garden well, one must appreciate plants and their different uses; and their associations with other growing things. A garden is always changing and one plants to make a better picture or to create, perhaps, another garden of herbs or roses without upsetting the original design. Changes are often forced: by a build-up of weeds; or because plants have outgrown their allocated space. To choose what you want to grow, and where, is not always immediately obvious. What do we want from our English gardens anyway?

Certainly, on a warm summer evening, we expect the romance of scents and misty colourings. We also admire, and many people are now making, what is called a 'natural' garden – the wild wood or wilderness which, believe me, is not suddenly achieved by just leaving the weeds to take over! Nevertheless, one can get a feeling of uncluttered simplicity just by careful planting. By allowing tall ornamental grasses, meadowsweet, cranesbill and moon daisies to grow and seed among good garden plants – many will themselves produce colonies and drifts of seedlings. If then they can be left undisturbed, they will merge into a controlled wild beauty. To many, this gives more satisfaction than traditional well-tended beds or borders of flowers. Midsummer is the time to think about these changes and to ponder what you can do in such-and-such a place or in that particular dark corner. In the evening, or early morning,

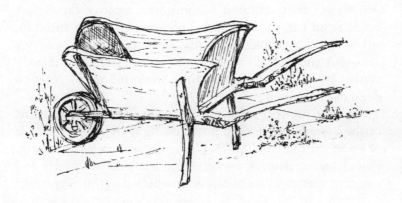

when the shadows give an illusion of space, one can often dream the dreams and see the visions of dramatic plantings. Even the birds' song helps!

A flower garden is not all romance and beautiful thoughts. There is the need to think positively if you are to carry out even the simplest of plans. Although it may not be obvious at first how to use your plants to the best advantage, making a romantic or artistic setting for them will help you to know what you want to plant and where. You may already have made, or have inherited, a garden of good design with which you are content. You then have only to enjoy keeping it well stocked with beauty. But to learn of, to hunt for and eventually find that special plant for that chosen place encourages a gardener's quest for good plants.

Many jobs can be done during the summer months in more leisure and comfort than in a hurry (whatever the weather) later. After supper on a warm evening, it is a joy to spend half an hour or so with secateurs and twine in the garden; you need not even change your shoes – but do take a wheelbarrow for those odd bits and dead heads that you might cut. As you wander, tuck in the current year's growth of the climbers and wall shrubs, tie in that unruly branch of pyracantha, shorten the new growths of chaenomeles to half their length, cut dead rose sprays back to a flowering bud to get more autumn blooms, and remove the flower heads from the sea kale and rhubarb. Pull up by the stalk any foxgloves or biennials that have set enough seed for next year and gently thin the peaches and some of the early apples. It is a peaceful occupation, so do not try to get it all done in one evening.

Another job that must not be overlooked is to cut some of the branches that have flowered right out from the base of some shrubs, leaving the young growth to take its place. Philadelphus, deutzia, some of the berberis, mahonias and rampant species of roses can be controlled in this way.

If you can get some of these jobs done as you admire your garden in the summer, you will have time in the autumn to search for, and find, something different for your newly designed garden.

Summer Pruning

OFTEN IN LATE SUMMER, it is easier to see what needs attention than when the branches are bare. So, recently, I was considering what should be done with some of the evergreen wall plants and shrubs which are crowding out others that need light and air. If some summer pruning is not done, there will be a lot of work in the autumn for, with so much rain, the shrubs can make tremendous growth. My grandfather's tale was that a dripping June kept all in tune, and certainly this does seem to be the case for the flower garden, with bright colours and everything lasting for such a long time. Even the delphiniums, though battered, stood until the very last flowertips as there were no strong winds. I always seem to be advocating the use of gravel and this year has proved my point: to be able to walk round the garden immediately after summer rain is one of the more pleasant moments of gardening.

The time to assess the needs of each shrub or plant is when it has finished flowering. You can then decide which branch is impeding the beauty of others or upsetting the balance of your whole design. A prostrate conifer that has sprawled too far over a path, a eucalyptus which needs thinning; *Osmanthus delavayi*, the jasmines, the different ham-amelis, *Fatsia japonica*, the species *Hydrangea* and even magnolias and the tree and moutan paeonies: none of these will be harmed if an offending branch is entirely removed now – not shortened or tipped or it will make more shoots where

you don't want them. Vines, roses, clematis and honeysuckles soon become spoilt with mildew if crowded; even
the camellias and rhododendron buds suffer. The summer
pruning of roses is something quite different, however, but
their needs are very simple: just cut back the branches or the
stems of individual blooms to a bud after flowering. If this
is not done, the result is leggy and sprawling plants with no
second flowering.

Garrya elliptica is already showing catkins at this time, so
it is too late to do much except remove any branch that is
really dead or in the way; but the fremontodendron will need
attention this month or its new growth will not stand the
winter. *Drimys winteri* and *Carpenteria californica*, the ceanothus group and *Cytisus battandieri* will all need a few branches
removed occasionally; all the variegated euonymus, elaeagnus and most of the viburnums soon get overcrowded. If
you have large plants of *Salvia purpurea* and *S. aurea*, rosemary, potentilla, sun roses, *Artemisia* 'Powys Castle', *Hebe*
'Pagei', and the hypericums, deal with them gently and they
will keep their shape and healthy texture into the autumn.
Another summer job is to remove with a small pruning saw
any dead branches on small ornamental trees: *Robinia pseudo-*

acacia 'Frisia' and *Catalpa bignonioides* 'Aurea' need it every year; the myrtles, abutilons and flowering cherries, even shrub roses, lilacs, conifers and crab apples must be watched – dead branches are not a pretty sight.

There is much that can be kept in good order by summer pruning, but do not tidy up too soon for there is all the leaf and berry colour to come later and the last clean up to the compost heap will come all too quickly.

As Summer Wanes

ANYONE CAN HAVE a garden full of colour in the spring. The most difficult time is later on in the summer, when the borders are becoming a little tatty and the autumn colours and fruits are two months away. That is when your grey plantings come into their own; and if you have managed some colour near your grey shrublets, you will now have a good substantial flower border that will last for weeks. It is important that such a planting should be watered in dry weather.

In August as the summer marches on, the tall-growing phormiums, *Crambe cordifolia*, and the giant Scottish thistle, *Onopordum acanthium*, seen against a wall or deep evergreen hedge, look lovely in the evening light. The giant hog weed, *Heracleum montegazzianum* is a joy in large gardens. It will easily reach nine feet and must be planted well at the back of everything, and kept there. All unwanted seedlings should be ruthlessly dug out when small, but I leave all the dead flower heads and bracts that I can, while tidying up: they will make another picture in October.

At this time of year, there will also be the tubs, pots and urns filled with half-hardy things you have held in the conservatory all winter, looking fresh and gay. In these containers, and near them, are geraniums, begonias, lilies, campanulas, Bowles' golden grass and the trailing dark-blue lobelia. So you have another three months of colour.

There are many compensations as summer passes and you

near the end of the growing season. In late August there will be pomegranate fruit on the south wall, the small strawberry guava in the conservatory will be ripe, the fruits of the medlar and the quince will look exotic – and you will be thankful that the abundant soft fruit is nearly over. But if the weather has been good the green figs will ripen daily, and it will be either you or the birds after them from daylight to dark!

August's Compensations

SO WHAT ELSE is in bloom, or about to bloom, in August? This is the time when we hear gardeners consoling each other about their lack of colour and how difficult it is to keep the garden looking healthy. Many neglected or weedy corners are more noticeable and if one tries to control bindweed or ground elder at this time it leaves the border in disarray for weeks. But as I go round my garden to count my blessings I find much that is lovely, despite the untidy verbascums and thistles with their dead flower heads: not least the butterflies on the buddleias and two baby hedge-hogs standing on an ants' nest having a good meal.

In August and September, purple is one of the best colours in the border. It can be used in so many different ways and goes well with the lime-coloured and silver-leaved plants that I recommended in *The Flower Border in August*, (page 84), the dark-leaved berberis and the purple nut, *Corylus maxima* 'Purpurea', *Rhus cotinus* (especially attractive with something pink nearby), the flower heads and leaves of *Phormium tenax* and *Sedum* 'Atropurpureum' with both purple stems and flower heads. The purple beech and *Acer platanoides* 'Crimson King' make a splendid backdrop for the light silvery branches of eucalyptus, silver birches and willow and also for the gleditsia and *Catalpa bignonioides* 'Aurea' which is at its best in August. But that is mostly background colour and beauty. What have we in flower in the border now? First, it must be *Romneya coulteri*, the tree poppy; and

then the yuccas, particularly *Y. filamentosa* which blooms each year; *Aralia elata*, the angelica tree; penstemons; blue and white agapanthus; the giant nicotiana and the grey-leaved Mediterranean shrublets of which there are too many to quote.

The largest splashes of colouring are *Hydrangea villosa*, *H. sargentiana* and *H. quercifolia* (see also *Late Summer Flowers*, page 89). All are hard-wooded and make large shrubs: *H. sargentiana*, for example, will grow to ten feet, among other shrubs, and does not mind some shade. *H. quercifolia* has oak-like leaves that turn a rosy colour in the autumn and, though called white in the catalogue, it can be a soft creamy colour. *H. villosa* is a lovely shade of pale mauve with woolly leaves; it just asks to be put next to something purple!

There is a lot of colour on the walls: not all flowers, certainly, but yards of *Hydrangea petiolaris* seed heads and the

pinky purple leaves of the *Clematis montana* 'Elizabeth'. Two
late-flowering clematis are at their best now: the strong
growing *C.* × *jouiniana* and the cowslip-scented yellow bell
flowers of *C. rehderiana*. Over the tool shed and reaching the
chimney pot of the boiler house is the golden hop which
gives us so much pleasure for so little attention: just cut it to
the ground when finished. Another exotic climber is campsis. We love our *C.* × *tagliabuana* 'Madame Galen' which is
no trouble if pruned back like a vine, but in April sends
sprays of orange-red bells through the branches of the
Magnolia grandiflora which is also in bloom at this time.

Many flowering bulbs start in August: the clivias, pink
and white; the nerines; the first hardy cyclamen. I must also
mention a few small plants, most of which are always with
us: rue, rosemary, lavender, lamb's ear, thymes and sages.
Although, as I have said, lists of plants are not much help
when making a garden, this must be an exception. How else
can I remind you of the lovely things you can grow in your
garden in August?

When Summer Ends

THE SUMMER OF 1988 is drawing to its close, the long summer evenings are over and it is dark at nine o'clock. Any time now, the first autumn gales will be with us. Although it has been dull and moist, it has been warm growy weather. The rain – and we have certainly had a lot – has been wonderful for the shrubs and border plants. They have put on a lot of new growth, and the flowers have been marvellous. There have been no high winds to batter the wet flower heads and everything has stood up well. There seem to have been fewer pests and only a little blight: an amazing amount of butterflies and moths, more ladybirds than usual, and so less green fly.

Although our evenings have not been completely taken up with watering, there has been no let up on the mowing, and the lawns have looked green and fresh all summer. The strawberries and raspberries suffered rather, but the blacks and the gooseberries cropped well; some apples were short because they didn't like the late frosts, but the late bloomers have given a lot of fruit. There has been a good picking of peaches, green figs – not yet ripe but a fair crop – a few quinces, and lashings of medlars.

If there were weeds – and we all have them – they were easy to pull up. So the old saying of a dripping June has been proved right once again. Everything has ripened late this year: the Victoria plums look well but are hard and green at the moment; the pears are like bullets. As yet, there are few wasps; perhaps because they hatched so late, they will be short of food and so fewer will come through winter. It may be because I am older, but the scents seem to mean more to me now than they did: even though we have lost the true scents of the mimulus and mignonette, the sweet peas and the roses smell as sweet as ever.

So, having reached September we have every excuse to relax by a log fire, dreaming of plans for next year, completing the seed lists and deciding that a wet year has its compensations after all.

The Colours of Autumn

THE AUTUMN – September, October and sometimes November – is a festival of fruit and colour, but not all the best pictures are man-made. The blackberry leaves in the hedges seem to turn a deeper purple than the cultivated ones, and with small clusters of wild honeysuckle fruits and old man's beard covering everything one wonders why one bothers to have a tame garden!

On the garden side of the hedge are fruits of sorbus, *Malus* × *robusta* and *M*. 'Golden Hornet', ornamental vines, the late seed heads of grasses and hydrangeas. The shrubberies are bright with branches of cotoneaster, pyracantha, the scarlet oak and some rose hips. From the top of the wall, down over a *Fatsia japonica* in full bloom, the last two clematis of the year, *C. orientalis* and *C. rehderiana*, reach the ground. The times of individual tree colours vary very much according to the soil and the environment you have created: our *Liquidambar styraciflua*, for example, does nothing until November and is then suddenly ablaze until the frosts. But the Judas tree, *Cercis siliquastrum*, cercidiphyllum, and the tulip tree *Liriodendron tulipifera* can all be depended on for good leaf colour, as can the cherries *Prunus subhirtella* 'Autumnalis', *P. sargentii* and *P.* 'Ukon' which were so glorious in flower in the spring. Silver-leaved trees are also most acceptable as the days shorten: pittosporums, rhamnus and the silver-leaved weeping pear are excellent and two wonderful silver conifers are *Abies concolor* 'Violacea' and *Cedrus atlantica* 'Glauca'.

Often when you least expect them, you will find fruits on trees, conifers and grasses: some are quite small and curiously shaped and marked: you should examine them very closely to see their delicate patterns.

In late autumn, when the weather is fine and warm and there is no wind, it often feels as if the leaves are waiting on tenterhooks for those first gusts to bring them tumbling down. Many people cannot abide leaves on the lawn or the paths and dash to clear them away to the compost heap, but they make just as good a mulch if pushed around the trees and shrubs where they fall. Enjoy everything while you can: winter is on its way!

October

An End and a Beginning

IN MANY WAYS, October can be thought of as the beginning of the gardener's year: nearly everything has stopped growing, most of the leaves are down and, with the rest of the garden refuse, safely tucked up as compost for next year. The lawn has had its last mowing – hopefully! – and the edges cut back where necessary to keep the curves exactly right; thankfully, the last runner beans and blackberries are in the freezer!

There are still a few jobs that are better done this month: the dahlias and the border chrysanthemums should be boxed up while you can still see their names; and if you have a greenhouse or warm shed in which to hold them, some of the culinary herbs – especially the mints – will come up much earlier than if left outside, but should be kept watered when growth starts. It is a good time to layer shrubs: choose a low branch, take a sharp knife and nick the branch just below a bud; peg down with a bent wire and you will have a good plant to be lifted in early spring when in leaf.

Before you put last year's compost around your shrubs and plants, and before you clean up and spray the greenhouse, you can with a clear conscience allow yourself time to relax and unhurriedly rearrange and plant what you wish and where; divide and move, plan and plant and replant, potter and dream; and put together those shapes and colours you thought would look well in the summer. Some of your perennials will have grown too large for their position and will now divide into good plants; if you do not want them for your new planting, put them in rows in your vegetable garden to give to friends or for a bring-and-buy stall.

The soil is usually just right in October for planting new trees and roses and not too sticky for walking on the herbaceous border. But do not forget to give everything you plant a big forkful of compost or, better still, farmyard manure. Trees and hedges should be in the ground and staked, without fail, in October. If your soil is well-drained they will only need to be planted snugly and well fed; but if on clay or a sticky wet soil, dig a much bigger hole than the plant, taking out some of the subsoil if necessary, and replace with top soil and peat, then mulch in the spring to encourage good root growth. All newly planted trees should be watered regularly if they are to make steady growth.

There are still many beautiful plants to enjoy in October. I have grown a batch of colchicums near *Sedum* 'Autumn Joy' and the small *Chrysanthemum parthenium* 'White Bonnet' with a silver-green *Yucca glauca* which is variegated and cabbage-like. Another rewarding mixture for October is *Ceratostigma griffithii*, commonly known as plumbago, and liriope backed by *Berberis thunbergii* 'Rose Glow'; and, in a damp place, that lovely plant with the dreadful name *Kirengeshoma palmata* is enchanting with acorn-like flowers on six-inch drooping stems. The sedums are wonderful in the autumn, for they last so long and the butterflies love their nectar – but first place must go, I think, to the nerines, for they withstand both wind and rain for weeks if planted under a sheltered south wall.

October is a lovely month, if fine, and midday is the best time to work outdoors. There may be still leaf and berry colour on that fine day. So enjoy a bite of cheese and apple outside but within sight of your wheelbarrow and fork. The robins will be noisily defending their territories and the blackbirds and thrushes interested in your freshly prepared soil. But don't be hurried. Gardening should be akin to 'messing about in boats': it is just being quietly happy as you put together your new planting.

Winter Beauty

WINTER BEAUTY starts for me at the first leaf fall, especially over farmland and countryside, for then the branches of poplar, birches and willow show up so well against the dark clouds and evening skies. The last tints on the hedges and lichens on tiled barns and old trees with the Downs floating above a line of river mist is something I remember all the year. So many lovely views are obscured by heavy tree shapes in the summer – now more than ever with so much conifer planting.

Another time of great beauty usually comes after Christmas when the ponds are frozen and, with or without snow, the grasses and reeds take on other forms, often glazed with frost and their seed heads drooping. If you have a man-made stream in your garden, the ground-hugging *Salix fargesii*, which has bright red pointed buds, and the bare branches of the cornus, if cut to the ground in April, make a splendid backcloth of winter colour when growing amongst stones as they would naturally at a water's edge.

The three months between autumn and spring, when the sun is low in the heavens, and there is little light or warmth, seems a long time to the impatient gardener, but in sheltered spots in most gardens there will always be something in flower. In very small gardens, one should be selective when using winter-flowering shrubs, for some have dull and uninteresting leaves in summer; but the bold dark *Garrya elliptica*, if out of the wind, followed by an April flowering

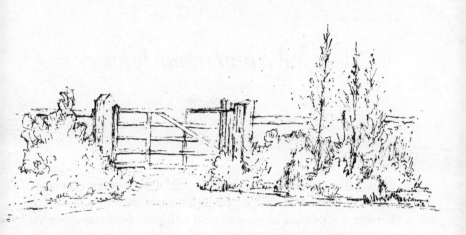

cherry with daffodils at its foot makes an inviting early picture.

If you have a mild spell in winter you can usually find the yellow winter jasmine, a few *Iris stylosa* and sprigs of *Sarcococca humilis* but to have *Hamamelis mollis*, both the wintersweets – *Chimonanthus fragrans* 'Grandiflorus' and *C. f.* 'Luteus' – *Sycopsis sinensis*, and sprays of *Daphne odora* and *D. collina* in full bloom is really heartwarming. The green winter *Helleborus foetidus* and *H. corsicus*, with a ground cover of the small variegated arum leaves, always make a wonderful picture – but with a few early snowdrops and clumps of golden aconites, it is even better. The autumn *Prunus subhirtella* has been in flower since November; and on a low wall is the spiky abeliophyllum which is so difficult to prune, but well worth the effort, for one small piece will fill a room with a fragrant scent.

Winter Scents and Flowers

LOOKING BACK through my garden diaries, I notice that so often there are a few open days of still weather at Christmas, perfect to go and find and pick the treasures that make up a glorious decorative Christmas arrangement. The hollies themselves are magnificent, with many of their leaves edged with silver or gold, some mottled or variegated. The colour of the berries differs almost as much as the foliage: on our thin soil, the berries are often not just red but dark almost to black. Traditionally, of course, with the holly go the mistletoe and the ivy. There are so many named ivies and they are so difficult to separate that, unless one is specialising, there seems no need to do so. Many of the gorgeous-leaved cultivars are only useful for large areas of wall or buildings, but there are some delicate, small-leaved varieties which are so easily controlled they can be used as ground cover, on house walls, or as pot plants. They have a flowery aroma of the outdoors which is very satisfying, but not to be compared with the delicate scent of a bowlful of winter flowers from the garden when brought into a warm room.

These treasures, which are a gardener's joy, must not be expected to flower until well established but, if correctly placed and well planted, will need very little attention. They will grow into beauty and last many years.

Many people give little thought to their gardens during the winter months, but in fact there is a lot going on.

Beautiful winter-flowering shrubs, so often scented, can be picked for indoor enjoyment in December and January and, in open weather, *Jasminum nudiflorum*, *Viburnum fragrans*, *V. × juddii* and *V. tinus* are closely followed by *Stachyurus praecox*, *Corylopsis pauciflora*, the mahonias and, of course, the Algerian *Iris stylosa*.

A really hard winter can be desolate and disappointing. The dreaded anticipation of the loss of valued plants, perhaps collected from their country of origin or gifts from friends, is with one all the time. Caring for a garden in the colder parts of Britain is a very different way of life than for those of us who live between the Downs and the sea, as at Denmans, but it is always a challenge and every year one takes risks, some calculated, some not. I remember particularly how by March 1985 we were still not sure what had survived the bitter weather we had had after the previous Christmas: with so little rain, the low temperatures played havoc with the hebes and Mediterranean plants we usually grow.

A hard winter is a testing time for gardeners, not only of their powers of ingenuity and careful husbandry, but also of their tempers, patience and faith in future undertakings. It is a pity to moan and grumble at the loss of plants, though it always seems to be something which has taken years to grow: perhaps you did not place it correctly, or the district wasn't suitable anyway. It might not be the weather at all: it could be you! So try again if you feel you must have it, for most plants can be replaced and a living garden is always changing anyway.

Postscript

AS I'VE SAID, most gardens are not made only for one year, or even for a specific length of time; there is always someone to follow who will be glad of your foresight. So what of Denmans' future? Denmans is a garden with a great potential, but a garden needs stability. It needs continuity of ownership or a settled future to give it the direction necessary for long-term planning. Fortunately, while horticulture is big business, there is also an upsurge of real garden lovers who are always seeking knowledge of plants and their uses, and ways of planting to suit their style of living. The future of Denmans lies safe in the hands of John Brookes, who lives in Clock House and who I hope will care for my garden during his lifetime; he is a grand garden maker. I asked what changes he envisaged for Denmans during his stewardship.

'I am often asked,' he said, 'what I will do with the garden when I am in charge of it – and point out that I have been running Denmans for the last three years.

'You don't move your life to a place you don't like – so there is no sense of waiting in the wings for an almighty upheaval at some distant date to give it a radical facelift. A garden is a continuing thing – it evolves slowly – and it would be foolish to suggest it will not change, but nothing I could envisage was half as radical as the effect of the great storm of October

1987. I think I have learnt from Joyce the value of planning ahead, but to a degree any foreseeable changes have to be reliant on maintenance and staff.

'So my primary objective is to create a small and responsible team to help me run what is becoming quite an operation – for I want Denmans to support itself. As a garden we are increasingly 'on the map'. To sustain this designation you need to service it with car-parking space, with refreshment and washing facilities, with a shop; and ideally a plant sales area as well, which in turn has to be serviced by propagating and holding space. All these facilities, with staffing, we now have.

'But the fabric of a garden which is nearly fifty years old needs constant attention and replacement too: timber rots, glass breaks, terracotta cracks and beautiful flint walls (considerably more than fifty years old) must be kept up to standard.

'All these priorities must be attended to before decorative development, though each winter we do undertake the re-appraisal of another area. I am fortunate in having the enthusiastic support of Simon Payne in charge of the garden, and at last I feel that I can be away from time to time without any disasters back home. In the long term I rather hanker after some small area of formality within the layout, to show that an integration with the organic movement of the rest of the space is possible. I would also like to find an instructional way of showing plants for particular places, without the effect looking too educational, since increasingly we have an informed audience passing through who are seeking advice and information.

'Plant naming is an ongoing sore point. Joyce has always maintained that this is a private garden, not a botanical one. Naming plants six or eight feet into a bed means huge labels and a full-time pair of hands to keep up with the job, and I intend to follow her precedent, only naming shrub roses as they come into flower, for instance, and other things of particular interest.

'Beyond this, it's a wait and see sort of situation. I am looking forward with an excitement that I hope will carry me into a contented though fulfilled future, within a lovely garden.'

INDEX

fuchsia, 19, 56, 90, 120, 121, 161

galtonia, 46
  G. candicans, 13, 85, 90
Garrya elliptica, 137, 148, 170, 184
gentian, 69, 91, 92
germander, 56
geranium, 19, 53, 56, 75, 92, 120, 121,
  172
Ginkgo biloba, 129
gladiolus, 13, 72
  G. byzantinus, 13, 46
  G. nanus 'The Bride', 86
gleditsia, 174
golden rod, 83
gourds, 75
gravel, gravel garden, 2, 12–13, 14,
  28, 46–7, 49–50, 53, 77, 119–20, 169
  dry gravel stream bed, 17–18
greenhouses, 52–3, 121, 160
guava, strawberry, 19, 173

hamamelis, 169
  H. mollis, 185
hawthorn, 79
heartsease, 50
heather, 109–10
hebe, 101, 132, 141
  H. 'Henri Defoss', 38
  H. hulkeana, 100
  H. 'Pagei', 86, 97, 170
Hedera helix 'Buttercup', 88
  H.h. 'Goldheart', 99
  H.h. 'Little White Diamond', 88,
  99, 148
Helianthus decapetalus 'London Gold',
  82
helichrysum, 76, 92, 97
  H. petiolatum 'Aureum', 19
hellebore, 47, 50, 63, 69, 87, 94, 96,
  117, 135, 138, 155–6, 164
  Helleborus corsicus, 96, 156,
  185
  H. foetidus, 50, 77, 185
  H. niger, 91–2
  H. orientalis, 77, 155
Heracleum mantegazzianum, 89, 172
herbs, 14–15, 51, 57, 132, 181

hibbertia, 19
hog weed, 172
holly, 58, 135, 136
hollyhock, 96
honesty, 74, 94
honeysuckle, 35, 56, 94, 97, 170, 179
  winter-flowering, 103
hop, golden, 32, 176
hornbeam, 131
hosta, 73, 85, 92, 113, 117
  H. decorata marginata, 38
  H. sieboldii, 38, 84
hyacinth, 13, 19
hydrangea, 89, 132, 169, 179
  H. arborescens 'Annabelle', 84
  H. quercifolia, 73, 87, 175
  H. petiolaris, 175
  H. sargentiana, 73, 87, 175
  H. villosa, 47, 73, 87, 175
hypericum, 170

insects, 60–1
iris, 18, 69, 86, 120
  Dutch, 11, 14
  flag, 83
  Gladwin, 46, 84
  I. stylosa, 67, 148, 155, 185,
  187
Itea ilicifolia, 85, 141
ivy, 53, 94, 99, 138, 155

Jasmine, 117, 169
  Jasminum nudiflorum, 187
  J. polyanthum, 53
  Tasmanian, 55
  yellow winter, 103, 148, 185
jonquil, 156
Judas tree, 179
kingcup, 94
Kirengeshoma palmata, 47, 182
Kniphofia caulescens, 89

lady's mantle, 31, 51, 73, 77, 83, 94,
  120, 163
Lagerstroemia indica, 56
lamb's ear, 83, 94, 176
Lamium, 18
Lathyrus latifolius, 74